Childhood Days

in

GLASGOW

by

Jenny Chaplin

First published in 1996 by

BUSINESSLIKE

'Bluepool', Strathoykel, ARDGAY, Sutherland, IV24 3DP

Tel: 01549 441211

ISBN 1 873572 19 0

CHILDHOOD DAYS IN GLASGOW

CONTENTS

CHILDHOOD DAYS IN GLASGOW

by Jenny Chaplin

ACKNOWLEDGEMENTS

The author acknowledges a debt of gratitude to the following:

1) My publisher/editorial director Iain McIntyre, 'BUSINESSLIKE Publishing', for his customary tact, patience, and professional expertise in guiding the MS safely into the light of day.

2) My husband, Capt. J. M. Chaplin M.N. (Ret'd), also a Govanite, who has walked with me for many a mile 'doon Memory Lane.'

3) Kinnon Enterprises, Winnipeg, Manitoba, Canada, for kind permission to include two poems from my Poetry Anthology, 'Alone in a Garden.'

4) Professor Manuel Linden, BA, MEIC, MCSME, FIED(UK), REng Des (UK) of Ontario, Canada, for his great kindness and humanity in sharing with me some of the memories, thoughts and beliefs culled from his own Glasgow childhood.

5) In the writing of this book, I have been at all times greatly encouraged by my local Librarian, Edward Monaghan, A.L.A. and his helpful staff at Rothesay Public Library. Eddie has urged me on to "tell it the way it was ... after all, Jenny, you lived in those conditions during that period of history." Here then ... single-end, mince-n-tatties, clootie dumplin, vinegar-rag, squeaky pulley, Lochgelly belt, Flannel Feet, Clyde launchings, High Heid Yins, fleas, Nit-Nurse, Liberty bodice, unemployment, caring community, Meenister o' the Kirk, Fever-van, sweet-bite dainties, Angel-scraps, peever, moshie, Scotch mutton pies, local flea-pit, extended family, loving parents, warts and all ... is the way it was.

INTRODUCTION

In 1994, 'BUSINESSLIKE Publishing' produced my 'TALES of a GLASGOW CHILDHOOD.' (ISBN 1-873572-13-1). This met with such wide and very welcome acclaim that, suitably encouraged, we now introduce this latest volume of additional childhood memories culled from life in the Glasgow of the Depression years.

The first book started when, at the tender age of eight years, I was conscripted to the 'advertising executive board' of Mac's Workmen's Restaurant in Govan's Elder Street.

The book now in your hands goes further back to 1928, when in a 'single-end' in a Glasgow tenement building, I first saw the light of day. Incidentally, a brief historical note here ... 'end' was the ancient Scottish word for 'a room in a cottage'. So a 'single-end' in a tenement building, far removed from anyone's ideal of a rose-embowered cottage, was taken to indicate a single-room ... and often a gey wee one at that!

But big or wee, the many millions of my generation who spent childhood days in such loving, if financially impoverished, homes throughout Britain, in the main, grew up to become responsible citizens. Compare the situation today!

As we approach the Millennium, in the society of today with its mass unemployment, poverty, violence, vandalism and avarice, many theories abound as to the reason for such ugliness.

The popular theory would appear to be that the root cause is that all criminals, and even minor wrongdoers, were the 'victims of deprived homes'. That being so, I thought the time was ripe to show that many millions of British citizens who grew up in the slums of Glasgow, Birmingham, Swansea, Belfast, Dundee, London, Cardiff, Edinburgh, Manchester - in what today would be described as 'deprived homes' - did not all grow up to become enemies of society.

Quite the reverse! In the main, we grew up to form the backbone of our country, and in the process, we became decent law-abiding, taxpaying citizens of Great Britain.

By and large, the people of my generation, lucky enough to have had jobs for life, worked hard, lived frugally and saved as many bawbees as we possibly could for the sake of a modicum of well-earned comfort in old age, with hopefully enough money left over to afford us a decent burial. Surely not too much to ask for a lifetime of endeavour, patriotism and in many cases, fighting for one's country?

And yet, with each passing year of higher and more stringent taxes, exorbitantly-priced main services and terror now stalking our once-peaceful streets, more and more of my long-suffering generation are being thrown on to the scrap-heap of society.

And having been what we Scots call "savin' bodies" all our lives, we pensioners now see ourselves being penalised for that very thrift, while others, perhaps less responsible in that area of their lives, are ushered as V.I.P. guests aboard the greatest 'freebie' of them all, namely the Benefits Gravy Train!

Having said that, we are however left with our memories! No-one can ever take those away from us. And to date, not even the most hated Government has as yet devised Value Added Tax on memories!

Memories are a precious, if often rather painful, commodity in anyone's life. And frequently we have only to hear mention of a par-ticular year, place, or historical event, in order to trigger off a whole series of vivid mental pictures - memories, one and all, be they happy, sad, or even downright traumatic!

Like many people of retirement age, I now find that one intrigu-ing aspect of getting older is that my memory tends to play strange tricks. For instance, ask me what I had for breakfast on any given morning, and I haven't a clue! However, as opposed to such faulty short-term memory, my mental pictures of people, events, years long since gone are crystal-clear.

This means that in common with millions of other Old Age Pen-sioners, I can describe with supreme confidence every single detail of my long-departed childhood. Yes! Can describe it down to the last shoe-button; the last game of 'peever'; or even down to the last sting of my teacher's stout Lochgelly belt as it crashed down on my chilblained hands over sixty years ago, when, as a 'Mixed Infant', I was being severely punished for having arrived late, 'efter ra bell', at Greenfield School in the Govan district of the 'Second City of the Empire.'

Yes! It's true! It's all ancient history now and a bygone age in which so many of us were dirt-poor, but since no interfering 'do-gooders' and their ilk thought to tell us that we were 'deprived', we lived happily enough in our impoverished homes, played safely in mean city streets, unencumbered by thoughts of child-molesters; and enjoyed the freedom, the collective discipline, the caring camaraderie of a close-knit and equally poverty-stricken community.

That was the reality of life for so many of us who did our growing-up in the Great Britain of the 1920's and 1930's.

Nowadays, living happily in retirement here on the lovely Island of Bute, hardly a day goes by but what I get a delightful letter from some far-flung outpost from loyal readers. They may have been brought up in a 'single-end' or a more 'upmarket' room-and-kitchen, but one and all, they each agree...

What we lacked in material wealth, was amply compensated by a caring, loving family environment in which not only did we get a wonderful training for life ... we came to appreciate that what really matters is the right set of moral values and above all else ... people.

Jenny Chaplin
Tigh na Mara Cottage
ROTHESAY
Isle of Bute
Scotland

A DISTANT MEMORY

When I was young
in the Glasgow of the thirties
I could walk the park in safety
I could wander to school
splashing through the puddles
my only fear?
of my teacher's Lochgelly belt
which would crash down on my hand
should I arrive
after the last peal of the bell
On arrival home
I'd get another beltin'
In this way I learned a new word-
not punctuality
but obedience-
obedience for life

A SINGLE-END IN GOVAN

The Glasgow of the 1990's, having achieved world-fame a few years ago, not in its old familiar guise as the home of poverty, depravity and drunken razor-gangs, but rather as a European City of Culture, is today a thriving, go-ahead, and above all, modern metropolis.

The Glasgow of the 1920's into which I was born, was such light years away, in every respect, that it might well have been on another planet!

Like so many Glaswegians of my day, I was born into a single-end, which is the name given in Scotland to a one-room flat in a tenement building and a home in which the entire family lived, ate, slept and had their whole existence.

I suppose that nowadays, given the addition of an en-suite bathroom, such a one-room home would be called a 'studio'. But, believe me, our single-end, in common with thousands like it throughout the length and breadth of Scotland, had no such luxury. So, what exactly did a single-end look like?

It had a black steel sink, more commonly called the 'jawbox', since, traditionally, Scottish housewives liked to 'jaw', blether or otherwise have a bit of a natter with friends and neighbours, while working at the sink which was invariably situated under the single window of the apartment; the sink boasted a goose-neck cold water tap; there was a 'press' or cupboard which did double duty as pantry and storage-space for pots and pans; a waxcloth-covered table; a bed set into the wall-recess; a patchwork quilt; lining the walls, strong wooden shelves laden with an assortment of guid weddin' china, inherited soup tureens large enough to hold sufficient Scotch broth to feed an army on the march, and chipped jumble-sale 'treasures' in the way of hideous and entirely useless ornaments; a black-leaded range with always on the boil, a pot of soup, 'stovies' or that great Scottish filler of empty bellies, namely porridge; a sawn-off nursing-chair for Mammy; a decrepit armchair for the Heid o' the Hoose; a crudely-fashioned wooden stool with a central finger-hole for ease of lifting; a gas mantle, our only source of light; a rough wooden bunker for the family's essential supply of coal; a squeaky overhead pulley on which was dried the family's washing; and centre of the home, the mantelpiece complete with crocheted fringe, the requisite pair of 'Wally Dugs', the guid weddin' knock which ticked away the seconds, minutes and hours of the family's life, an ornate tea-caddy with its own special spoon inscribed: 'A Wee Present Frae Bonnie Dundee', and standing like sentinels at each end of the mantelpiece, a pair of brass candlesticks.

That then was the physical setting and detail of virtually any single-end in the whole country of Scotland in the 1920's and 1930's.

And where exactly was our particular single-end? It was situated in a greystone tenement building in Langlands Road, in the Glasgow district of Govan, a formerly busy and thriving little community, then world-famous for its shipbuilding.

Close on seventy years ago, the accepted form of transport was the tramcar, horses and carts trundled over cobble-stoned streets, and each night, wee, bowlie-legged Leerie, with his long pole, would light the gas lamps in the streets of Govan.

The gas-lamps would have been alight early on December 22nd 1928, one of the shortest days of the year, and the day on which I was born. Inside our single-end home, my poor Mother, who had been in the agonies of labour for thirteen hours, must have felt the day to be endless. She was being attended in her hours of travail by a kindly, well-meaning but otherwise unskilled neighbour, who was by her way of it, every bit as competent as the official local Midwife!

This worthy did her feeble and inefficient best to help my Mother in her long hours of trial. This she did by mopping at my Mother's brow with a vinegar rag, and all the while quoting what she, in her wisdom, thought to be appropriate words of comfort from the 'Guid Book.' As well as being given to such Bible-thumping, the would-be Midwife also, throughout her ministrations and readings, used as a sort of Greek chorus the promise that all would eventually be well, for it was well known that:
"Joy cometh in the mornin'.
Joy cometh in the mornin'."
In the end, it wasn't Joy and it certainly did not come in the

morning! Like most expectant parents, my Mother and Father had previously chosen the names they would use for their off-spring. In the manner of such decisions, there had been much heart-searching as to wondering which relatives and in-laws would be least offended if their names were not chosen. In the good old Scottish tradition, many girls were named after Grandfathers and were thus condemned to go through life as Donaldina, Jamesina, Williamina. Such names of course lent themselves well to being shortened, a custom which my Mother disliked, having variously been called Jinty, Jenny or Jen, instead of her

Joy cometh in the morning

given name of Janet. Anyway, my parents finally decided on names which not only, they hoped, would be difficult to shorten, but they were names which they themselves liked. Even if it meant living with the fact that they would never inherit an offended Aunt Euphemia's guid 'wally dugs', nor even Uncle Archibald's tin of war medals, the final decision had been made. It would be Hugh Telfer, after my Father, for a boy, and strangely enough, Joy for a girl!

However, by the time I made a somewhat belated appearance into this world from whatever realms I had previously been inhabiting, it goes without saying that my Mother, heartily sick of listening to the midwife going on about 'Joy', never wished to hear the accursed word again!

So, for speed, convenience and in an effort to resolve the matter, Mammy agreed that I should be called after her. Thus, without further ado, my father was despatched to register the birth.

No doubt, Mammy with a sigh of relief then snuggled down under the patchwork quilt, happy in the knowledge that her own little Janet had arrived safe at last, with the requisite number of fingers and toes and was so soon to be labelled for life. And Mammy had probably already decided that her wee girl would have her 'Sunday-name' at all times ... she for one, would never allow the lovely name to be shortened or otherwise messed about.

Meanwhile, back at the Registry Office, my father was obviously still in a high old state of excitement. So much so that, in a moment of mental aberration, he gave the name as 'Jenny.' Oddly enough, the same fate befell a friend of mine, meant to be named after her mother, Margaret, who instead ended up labelled for life as 'Maggie.'

And back in that single-end, poor Daddy's reception after his child-naming efforts, can best be left to the imagination of the reader!

Early on in my upbringing, Mammy decided that hampered with a sawn-off apology for a name or not, nevertheless, she would do her level best to rear me to become a decent citizen. Above all else, she did not want me ever to become a Glesga Keelie.

Many were the 'skelpit letherins' I got to my small bare bahookie in an attempt to cure me of my naughtiness, my jealousy and my temper tantrums. Although I myself still have but a hazy recollection of this early phase of my life, such was not the case with my dear Mammy. The memory of this well-deserved and appropriately-administered chastisement to her first-born, nagged and worried at my Mother's mind right up until the day she died. And this, despite my oft-repeated assurance that it was "all right."

I must have told her hundreds of times to put it out of her mind. It was past. It didn't matter. And anyway, the smackings must have done me some good, for in all humility, I can claim to have grown up into a God-fearing, law-abiding, decent member of society.

In becoming a decent citizen, it would appear that eventually I did fulfil Mammy's hopes and dreams for her wee family. Even today, I can still remember how often, in old-age, Mammy would delve back into the past, apologise to me yet again, and then finish with the words,

"Of course, I was only young myself, Jenny. I was jist a lassie of nineteen when you were born. I was trying to bring you and your brother up weel. All I ever wanted was for you baith to grow up into decent citizens. I didnae want you to become Glesga Keelies."

A 'Glasgow keelie' is the phrase generally used to denote a hooligan, the scum of the earth, an unwashed member of the lower orders of society. While it is true that the famous writer, Jack House once dedicated a book to "The salt of the earth - the Glasgow keelie"; I think there is no doubt as to which interpretation Mammy put on the words!

MINCE-N-TATTIES

I was just a month short of my third birthday when we had an addition to the family. Having had such a bad time in bringing her first-born into the world, Mammy was taken into hospital for the second birth.

Strangely enough, my recollection of the first sight of my wee bree, Telfie, is somewhat dim. All I do remember is that from having been the one and only adored child, I was suddenly cast in the role of Mammy's helper, a general 'goafer', who was expected to fetch and carry everything from talcum-powder to safety-pins for the comfort of a screaming, red-faced bundle in whom I had but a passing interest and who, right from the moment of his baptism, had gone one better than me in getting what I privately called a 'proper' name. His full name, what we in our family called his 'Sunday' name, was Hugh Telfer McCracken, which to my young mind, at least, was a million times better than my own sawn-off apology for a name.

The fact that my wee bree became generally known as 'Telfie' may well have had something to do with my own dark feelings of sibling rivalry and embittered jealousy!

In later years, Mammy explained to me that before my brother was born, she herself had spent long hours at our local Elder Park Library, a magnificent library just across the road from us which had been opened on 5th September, 1903, by none other than the famous Andrew Carnegie. Any bits of history like that were seized upon by my father who never missed an opportunity to educate me in Scottish social history. One wonders what my hugely pregnant mother had been studying in the library. She had taken it upon herself to wade her way through all the 'right' books which dealt with the rearing of children. Apparently, those pioneers in child psychology advised that the best method to use in order to avoid sibling jealousy and/or rivalry was to make the older child feel 'useful'. The idea was the 'useful' one would at once realise that he/she was an important, vital and highly valued member of the new set-up, right from the first command.

Well, the theory may have worked splendidly with other children, but whichever psychologist worked out that little gem of wisdom, obviously got it seriously wrong in my case! From the moment that I clapped eyes on the little interloper into my previously cosy and self-centred life of an adored only child, I regarded him as a pest ... and that with a capital 'P.'

The fact that he all too soon developed into an angelic-looking child with soft, golden curls, while I, previously the star of the show, was can-can straight, moosey-broon, tubby and front-toothless into the bargain, did nothing at all to halt sibling rivalry when it first reared its ugly head. Quite the reverse, in fact!

The first really clear memory I have of childhood is that of a winter's day when I was sitting in front of a roaring fire, at which I was happily toasting my knees. I was seated at a toy table, which Daddy had made and which, to us, was more valuable than the Honours of Scotland.

The meal we were about to have was my favourite, a nice mushy helping of mashed potato, cabbage and mince. Having a few days previously been dared to jump down a flight of stairs I was now minus all my front teeth. So, anything soft to eat for a 'gumsie' like me, most definitely got my seal of approval. As far as Telfie went, however, it was an entirely different matter!

The far-off sounds of a dog barking, a tram-car screeching as it rounded the corner at Elder Street; even the cries of other children in the tenement building were muted and remote from us. Sealed in, as we were, by the fog, from the cold and misery of the streets of Govan, we were cosy and isolated in our own little world. It was a tranquil, happy, domestic scene in our poor, but spotlessly-clean little home. That was until Telfie got started!

Mammy had spent the morning on her knees, polishing, scrubbing, dusting, while with every minute, the stench and dirt of the fog was negating her every action. For all that, the ritual Friday cleaning was over for that week.

The mid-day meal for Telfie and myself had been set out on our toy table by Mammy, before she herself sat down with a sigh of relief at a job well done. With an enamel mug of tea and condensed milk in one hand, she rested her other arm along the length of the waxcloth-covered table at which she sat.

I can still see the scene in that room, Mammy wearing her dust-cap, her work-worn hands for once idle and the meal set before us weans. On Telfie's plate, as on mine, was piled a mound of creamed potatoes, an even greater mountain of boiled cabbage and some gravy, which with its countable specks of meat, was rather euphemistically called 'mince.'

Now, Telfie loved potatoes in whatever shape or form, would grandly condescend to choke down a few spoonfuls of 'mince' without too much boaking and retching, but there he drew the line! He would not, under any circumstances, put tooth to cabbage!

Since I, in my usual role of Mammy's valued helper, was in charge of the little pest, it was thus my duty to coax, cajole or otherwise threaten him with dire consequences such as the 'Bad Fire' should he refuse to 'eat up his cabbage.'

Telfie would squirm, cry and retch himself into a sorry state over a plateful of spinach, which he only mildly despised. When it came to his pet hate of cabbage, then we really were in trouble!

He manfully waded his way through the mashed, creamed potatoes, spooned up the gravy after first having syphoned off the specks of minced meat, and had finally rearranged the cabbage into a pleasing, artistic shape. That done to his entire satisfaction, he then clattered the spoon onto his plate, with a certain panache and a decided air of finality!

With a sigh of resignation, a silent prayer to whichever saint looked after big sisters with recalcitrant wee brees, and little hope in my heart, I prepared to do battle. I employed all my previously tried and tested ploys to encourage him. I divided the now cold cabbage into sections and invited him to:

"Jump the big river and get the magic cabbage before the horrible giant comes along and steals it for his greedy self!"

Quite a clever strategy, one might have thought? Judge for yourself how bright it was when you hear Telfie's considered reply to such an invitation: "Jenny! Telfie no' like magic cabbage! Let the big giant eat it all. Telfie no' like magic cabbage."

The wee pest never said a truer word, for he detested cabbage with every fibre of his being, whether it was magic cabbage or any other variety! But still I knew that I had to persevere. So, I then told him that cabbage would make him big and strong. Yes! And here I really let my imagination have full sway ... he would even become a mightier man than good old Popeye himself! Yet again, Telfie had his answer ready; "But Telfie wants to speak funny and be strong like Donald Duck. And he not eat cabbage!"

And nor, it seemed, would Telfie eat cabbage. To make doubly sure of that, he slammed the plate to the edge of the table. It teetered there for all of a second, frozen in time. Then, over it went. The plate crashed to the floor, scattering cabbage over a wide area of newly-polished linoleum. Telfie's look was one of joy. Mine, one of horror!

The crisis for him was over. Mine was just beginning. I knew well from past experience whose bare bottom would be at the receiving end of yet another skelpit letherin'.

I had, yet again, failed in my duty to 'look efter the wean', so retribution would follow. With a sigh of resignation - this time I did not even bother to invoke the celestial care of any hovering saints - I removed from my knicker-pocket my carefully-hoarded chunk of puff candy. As I laid this delicacy down on the table, well out of the reach of Telfie's sticky fingers, I noticed that pieces of fluff were sticking to my favourite sweet-bite. However, there was no time to do anything about the puff candy right at that moment. Other, more immediate and more urgent matters awaited.

"Telfie no' like magic cabbage"

I started to peel off my navy-blue velours and rolled up my Liberty Bodice for greater ease of access to my small bare bahoochie. By now I knew the drill well!

FLANNEL-FEET'S ON THE RAN-DAN

The street lamps had been lit and the jets from the gas flickered and cast their shadows on the gleaming wet pavements as I picked my way over the puddles and mounds of dogs' dirt. When I reached the gable-end of the tenement, I hesitated for a minute at the tram-stop. Still clutching the penny in my hand, I bit at my lower lip as I debated whether or not to do exactly as Mammy had told me. But another tantalising whiff from my precious package and the promise of an entire pennysworth of puff-candy for Monday's play-piece, soon made up my mind for me. Squaring my shoulders, I set off at a brisk pace, meaning to do the journey in record time, and, meanwhile clearing my conscience by telling myself that there was no sign of any yellow tramcar coming anyway.

There was a huddle of men hanging about the street corner and I glanced at them as I passed. In the normal way, I would never have given them a second glance, but what with the day's events, together with Betty Cameron's recent horrific stories about 'Flannel Feet' being on the loose again, I thought it best to keep my eyes and ears open.

As if seeing these men for the first time, my eyes took in every detail of their appearance. Like a uniform, each scarecrow of a man wore a long white, fringed scarf, a thin black suit and, like a badge of office, a flat tweed bunnet. To a man, their hands were thrust deep into the pockets of their hand-me-down suits and the only apparent movement was from their feet which shuffled back and forward, back and forward endlessly. To me, it seemed as if those restless feet had a life of their own and were willing the men to go somewhere, anywhere; were urging them to try something, anything to relieve the monotony of their lives and take them as far away as possible from the streets of Govan. As I passed, no-one spoke, whistled or acknowledged my presence in any way whatsoever. In fact, I would doubt that they were even aware of my presence, for each man wore his bunnet straight on his head with the skip pulled low over his forehead. With the canny, inborn instinct of the slum child, I knew better than to disturb those men. True, there would be neighbours lurking under those bunnets,

17

but I had no right to look into their eyes.

Far better to leave them to whatever peace they could find, for under such shelter could be seen no poverty, no empty shipyards, no rat-infested tenements and no shawl-clad women grown old before their time with the double burden of too many weans and never enough siller for food with which to fill their empty bellies.

Suddenly our peace was shattered. The door of "The Wee Man" was crashed back by an unseen hand and a beam of light sliced the darkness. Raucous sounds issued from the pub as a chorus of voices shouted encouragement to the pair of giants now locked together and battling in the doorway. Always mindful of Mammy's words of warning, I tried to hurry on past, but just at that moment, Mr. McWhirter managed to grasp the drunk by the scruff of the neck and with one almighty shove sent him hurtling out into the raw October night.

With a dull thud, a yelp of pain and a mouthful of obscenities, some of which even I, street-wise as I was, had never before heard, he landed in the gutter, right at my feet. With a sharp intake of breath, I looked down at him where he lay, a stinking, swearing, blubbering caricature of a man. Some of his words were lost to me, but in spite of myself, I found that I was straining to hear. I caught the last of his words: "No' ma bloody fault ma money's done, is it? Fairfields'll no' gie me ony work. And noo that auld bastard'll no' gie me ony booze. Whit a bloody, f---' life, int'it?"

I gasped at the sound of *that* word which Mammy had said time and time again must never be used by any of her family, and this despite the fact that it seemed an integral part of the daily speech of many Govanites. The sound of my gasp of horror had obviously penetrated his alcoholic haze, for the drunk raised his head and finding himself with a captive audience, fixed me with a bleary eye and slobbered,

"See him? See that f-----' bastard, hen? That's a' he is. A big, fat, blood-suckin' bastard. Ah'm Ah no' richt, hen? Eh?"

I kept my mouth firmly shut and at the same time, heart hammering in my chest, I tried to sidle past. But drunk or not, the man was too quick for me. As if throwing a mooring line, his arm shot out into the darkness and his fingers closed tight around my ankle. For a second, I gazed in fascinated horror at the filthy fingers grasped around my white ankle-sox. Then, summoning all my strength, I yelled as long and as hard as I could. At this, a few men on the opposite corner pushed back their bunnets and one man yelled, "Heh! Wullie! Leave ra wean alane. Ya big eejit. If ye're wantin' a barney, pick oan sumbody yer ain size, for Christ' sake."

The only effect this had on the drunk was to make him try to get to his feet. Still keeping a grip on me, he heaved his body along the gutter and with his free hand, and all the while grunting like an animal, he grovelled about in the puddles as if seeking something of value which he had lost. At last, with a final grunt of satisfaction, he withdrew a sodden object from where it had become lodged in the iron grating at the edge of the gutter. He shook the limp rag a couple of times and then rammed it onto his head. He seemed to draw some inner strength from the wearing of his bunnet, for he at once appeared to grow in both stature and confidence. Shoving his face close to mine, he said, "Therr! That's better noo! Thinks he's a big man, does he? Weel, Ah'm gonnae show him sumthin' that'll pit his gas in a bloody peep. Ah'm twice the man he'll ivver be, so Ah'm ur."

That speech finished, he delivered himself of a gargantuan belch. Then, a slightly puzzled frown on his ugly face, he leaned even closer to me and slavered, "Here! Lissen, hen! Issat chips Ah'm gettin' a wee niff o'?" Without waiting for my reply, he slapped his free hand against his thigh, in an ecstasy of delight and roared, "By God, an' it is! Is this no' ma lucky day? A poke o' chips shoved under ma snoot for free. Aye, an a nice wee lassie like yersell tae feed me. My, and things is ferr lookin' up. Gie's a chip, hen, that'll dae me for the meenit. We'll get tae the other wee treat later, don't you worry aboot that, ma wee chookie."

The fumes of the alcohol were in my nostrils and the stench of stale booze and vomit sickened me and made me retch. Even so, and all the while boaking my heart up, with one last superhuman effort, I sucked the fetid air into my lungs and bawled in a frenzy of hysteria,

"Mammy! Mammy! Ah want ma Mammy!"

As my cries echoed in the night air, just then I heard a voice yell out from over the road, "Wullie! Heh, Wullie! For the love o' God, leave ra wean alane! Ye'd better let her go. Or you'll be the wan for the high jump. An it's no' her Mammy neirrer ye'll huv tae worry aboot. Ye daft gowk! D'ye no' ken? Her Granfaither's Auld Mac hissell!"

At these words, the drunk suddenly changed tactics, but not as yet the hawser-like grip on my arm. The stinking breath came even closer, as with an ingratiating grimace, he simpered and whispered in a whisky-hoarse voice, "Auld Mac! Issat a fact? Weel, Ah'll tell you somethin' darlin'. Jist so happens Ah'm a big pal o' Auld Mac's, so Ah'm ur. An Ah'm gonnae gie his beautiful, luvly, darlin' wee grand-wean a nice big, shiny, silver sixpence, and....." His face clouded with the sudden realisation of the paucity of his current financial state. He plunged his free hand into his coat pocket and then as he dropped his other hand to continue the search, I made good my escape and took to my heels.

Already hopelessly late, I opted to ignore yet another of Mammy's oft-repeated admonitions and thus headed at high speed straight across the patch of dimly-lit waste-ground which was the quickest route home. Clutching my by now lukewarm package, and looking neither to right nor left, I raced across the cinder path as if 'Flannel Feet' himself were hard on my heels. I ran and didn't stop running until I had reached the comparative safety of our own close-mouth. Arrived there, I leant against the dank wall of the entrance and still heaving and panting, as much from terror as from the actual physical act of racing like a gazelle, I tried to get my breath back. I was still taking great gulps of the cat-pee and urine-infested air when suddenly an unseen hand jerked open a door in the close. I jerked my head up, expecting to see the enquiring face of Mammy and instead found myself looking into the rheumy eyes and wizened face of Auld Granny McGuinness. With a wicked gleam in her watery eyes, the old woman said, "Aye, Ah thocht Ah heard sumthin. Ah micht huv knew it wid be you, Jenny McCrack-en. Whit's up wi' ye noo? If it's no wan thing it's anurrer. If ye're no' annoyin' ra life oota that wee darlin' brither o' yours, then ye're up tae some ither daft cantrip. Whit's up? Flannel Feet get a haud o' ye, did he?"

With lips pressed together, I sidled past Granny towards my own front door. All the while, I could feel Granny's eyes boring into me, but determined not to give her the satisfaction of a reply, I kept my eyes rooted to the ground.

Giving the thin plywood of our front, and only, door a hefty kick with the toe of my best school shoes, I then put my mouth to the shining brass letter-box and bawled out, "O-PEN, Mammy! O-PEN! It's me! O-PEN."

When I was finally admitted, after what seemed an age, with Granny all the while boring venomous thoughts into the back of my skull, I was at first lost for words. I could hardly believe that I was safe at last and when I entered my home, the snug comfort, familiarity and cosy warmth of the single-end enveloped me. Not so Mammy's welcome!

"Jenny! Jist where the devil huv ye been? Ye've been oota the hoose for near an hour, so ye huv. An' pair wee Telfie here's ferr stervin', so he is. Been greetin' sair for his chips since the meenit ye went oota that door."

I hung my head and toed patterns in the linoleum, all the while playing for time to work out my best strategy. At length, I proffered the soggy package and said meekly, "Ah'm sorry, Mammy. It wisnae ma fault. Weel, ye see, for a stert .... therr was a ... a queue ... aye, that's it .... a queue, a great big, enormous queue at the Chippie's ... and.."

Before I could finish my fairy tale, poor starvin' wee Telfie took up the cry, "Chippies! Chippies! Me want chippies!"

Mammy turned to her second-born and said, "Weel, wee yin, ye're gonnae huv tae haud oan for a minnit or twa yet. They're stone cauld." So saying, she snatched the package away and bustled over to the black-leaded grate. Then turning to me, she scowled and with a questioning tone in her voice, went on,

"A queue, eh? Is that whit ye're tellin' me? Weel, that's as may be. But even so, Jenny......."

I blushed and at once started to protest. "It's true, Mammy! Honest! Cross ma herrt and hope tae die. And then when Ah came oota ra Chippie's, Ah couldnae get oan a caur .... the first wan wis ... er ... fu' up. Aye, it wus bung full, Mammy! Honestly! And then it took .... weel, forbye, it took ages for anurrer yellow caur tae come.

Ye ken whit that number seevens is like, Mammy! Ye said it yersell last time we went tae visit Auntie Mima in Brigton."

Mammy left me standing in an agony of uncertainty while she leisurely poked the fire and then straightened up the chipped enamel mugs on the oil-cloth covered tea-table. Finally, she gave me a piercing look and I was forced to go on, "Weel, honest, Ah could huv walked quicker, Mammy. But ye tellt me tae be sure an get the caur, seein' as it wus Friday nicht and that. So Ah jist .... jist waited, Mammy. And Ah mind tae whit ye tellt me aboot nivver taking a short cut ower the Dump, eirrer day or nicht. So... Ah jist waited, Mammy."

"Oh! Ye did, did ye? Weel, Ah'm richt gled for tae hear that ye're beginning tae dae whit yer Mammy tells ye. That's a guid girl."

I breathed a mental sigh of relief and gave Mammy my most ingratiating smile. For one terrified moment, I wondered if I had rather overplayed my hand, for Mammy gave me one of her 'special' looks and muttered something under her breath about my being 'gey flushed' for somebody who'd jist spent hauf the nicht hangin' aboot a tram-stop waiting for a yella caur.

But in that moment, I knew. I knew that come what may, there would be no pennyworth of puff-candy for Monday's play-piece after all. Even if Mammy didn't find the contraband copper on my person, my conscience would dictate that I give my ill-gotten gains to Miss Ferguson at Sunday School for the eventual benefit of the poor, starving children who lived in terrible conditions in the faraway-across-the seas land of Africa. After all, I was one of the lucky ones and I'd had an even luckier escape, both in getting away safely from that drunk man and in dodging from a potential life of crime. Yes! I was one of the lucky ones..... I lived not in the hell-hole that must surely be Africa... I lived in the Govan of the Depression Years. Just how very fortunate could one rather foiled, frustrated, but nevertheless thankful young cub-criminal be? As I reached the end of my ritual saying of "Gentle Jesus Meek and Mild" on that particular night, I offered up a little extra of my own composition to the effect that I was glad to be "Jist a Wee Glesga Girl - and forbye, I'd be a guid girl."

THE HIGH HEID YINS

As a child growing up in the adult-oriented climate of the 1930's, my life seemed to be ruled inexorably by a motley crew of people in authority. These were commonly referred to as 'the High Heid Yins' and included such authoritarians as Mammy, Daddy, the Heid Maister, the School Doctor, the Panel Doctor, the Infants Mistress, the Nit Nurse, the Parkie, the Jannie, the Meenister, the Elder Park Librarian, and of course, not forgetting that ever-present Scottish phenomenon, namely, the Queen o' the Close.

Living in a Glasgow tenement meant many things, not least that to reach one's home, it was necessary to walk through the common entrance, known to all and sundry as 'the Close.'

No matter what assortment of characters each building contained, be they clean, honest, God-fearing families, or those of the 'durty wee midden' variety, nevertheless every Close had one ... a Queen of the Close!

This unique phenomenon was a self-appointed position and one of great prestige, authority and importance. The Queen of the Close took it upon herself and her broad shoulders to prevent legless drunks from using the common entrance either as an open-air, draughty 'cludgie', or a convenient 'doss-house;' to 'check' or otherwise castigate cheeky, unruly children; to scare off stray cats and dogs and hopefully prevent them from bespoiling the doorsteps and coconut mats of a generation of proud, hardworking Scottish housewives; to see that the rota of stair-washing was strictly adhered to; to sweep into the back-court middens the previous night's accumulation of fish-and-chip newspapers and other even more unsavoury rubbish; to ensure that the pipe-clayed and ornate pattern, always so lovingly and expertly executed around the perimeter of the close, was kept looking pristine; to see to it that no housewife ever had the audacity to jump the queue in the oft-disputed matter of whose "turn it was to hing oot the washing" in the back-court; and at all times to keep a weather-eye on the comings and goings of all visitors, uninvited guests and other such unauthorised personnel to the building.

It was not only in the poorer districts of the City that a Queen of the Close reigned supreme and ruled her subjects with an iron hand, and that usually minus the velvet glove!

Many years later in adulthood when I aspired to living in an upmarket 'Wally-close' in Glasgow's posh West End, I felt quite at home on the very day of my promotion to the upper strata of society.

What happened was that my furniture removal man, with perhaps rather more brawn than intelligent brain had inadvertently broken a window on the half-landing of the close as he battled his way upstairs with a chest-of-drawers. He was at once taken to task by a formidable matron, what I would call a 'strong Madam', and one who, in the uncanny tradition of her breed, as though with some sort of inborn radar system, materialised from out of the ether, all set to do battle! Yes! you've guessed it! No matter how posh the district, nor even how 'pan-loaf' the accent, every tenement had one, that guardian of the common entrance - the Queen of the Close.

Another 'strong madam' who took a hand in training me in the way I should go as a child was the Librarian of our local Elder Park Library. This stickler for discipline not only insisted on funereal quiet within the sacred confines of the hallowed building, she regarded it as her God-given right to inspect the cleanliness, or otherwise, of would-be readers to the Junior Library. This woman instilled such terror into me that on at least one occasion, I had to flee the cleanliness line-up in order to give my grubby hands another washing. On those days of hurried departure, I had to run hell-for-leather and hope to make it to the nearest 'cludgie', in time before fair 'burstin' and in a high old state of anxiety, I would disgrace myself forever and 'streamie' all over the library floor!

And as for the Parkie in nearby Elder Park, many a confrontation I had with him also. To our childish eyes, the Parkie simply made up the rules for the sheer hell of it, to suit himself and at the same time, rid himself of squads of noisy, over-exuberant, snotty-nosed weans.

However, it is only in retirement, some sixty years later, that I came across an old book which, in detailing the opening of the Park in 1885, also gave a list of the Bye-Laws. These Bye-Laws of the Elder Park, Govan, had been confirmed by none other than His Grace, the

Duke of Richmond and Gordon, the then Secretary for Scotland.

In studying at least some of the 26 Rules and Regulations, it is apparent that as a wee Govan lassie, I must have broken at least a score of them! Nae wonder that the Parkie was forever bawlin' the odds at me and my pals! Judge for yourself:

"No person shall enter or leave the Park except by the ordinary gates." So much for the times we squeezed through any convenient gap in the railings!

"No person shall, in the Park, commit any nuisance or annoyance to any person using the Park." What about the times we hounded young lovers seeking a bit of peace and quiet!

"No person shall wade, wash, bathe or fish in the lake." Nae wonder a purple-faced Parkie chased us when we paddled, washed our stinkin' feet and finally trawled with a penny-net for 'baggy-minnows.'

"No person shall, within the Park, throw or discharge any stone, snowball or other missile." 'Nuff said on that score!

Mammy, of course, was the greatest High Heid Yin o' the whole banjing. As I recall it, she was always full of good advice ... and not least in the matter of teeth-rotting sweeties, chocolate bars, toffee-apples and coconut tablet.

A MacCallum "pokey hat"

All Glesga weans had a very sweet tooth and in this I was no exception in that I too ate my way through mountains of puff-candy, toffee-balls, Barrett's sherbet dabs, liquorice-straps, bubble-gum, ogo-pogo eyes, conversation lozenges, jelly-babies, tablet, slices of clootie-dumplin, fresh-off-the griddle 'pang-cakes', and all washed down with libations of lemonade, otherwise known as 'ginger' by Glesga weans, and not forgetting 'sugarollie-water.' The latter delicacy was made, usually when sitting in the back-court, by the simple expedient of shaking small pieces of liquorice in a bottle of water ... not exactly the most hygienic of operations, but the resulting brew was always delicious!

Another favourite delicacy was that of a pokey-hat, in other words, an ice-cream cone. Even better if one could afford to spend carefully-hoarded pocket-money on a 'MacCallum'. This was ice-cream with a mouth-watering raspberry-sauce poured over it. As a child it never once occurred to me to question how or why this sweet-bite got its name. To me, MacCallum was just that and nothing more. It was close on sixty years later that I learned the history. Apparently the whole idea of the raspberry-sauce poured over the ice-cream was an early form of advertising! It seemed that a Mr. G. MacCallum, who was a keen supporter of Clyde Football Club and wanting to promote his team's colours, he persuaded his local ice-cream seller to squeeze the red liquid over the top of his pokey-hats. The rest is history!

Readers will be aware that in detailing a list of High Heid Yins, such characters as the Heidmaister, oor teachers and the Jannie have been allotted their rightful place in the chapter about schooldays, entitled 'A Pair o' Purple Breeks.' As for our loving and ever-supportive grandparents, they, in the way of all grandparents worthy of the name, were the ones who spoiled us rotten. As such, and as the providers of all manner of teeth-decaying sweet-bites, they were not lumped into our mental classification of 'High Heid Yins'. Having said that, however, their word was still law and it would have been a gey glaikit wee Glesga keelie that ever got on the wrong side of any iron-hand-in-a velvet-glove Granny or Grampa! We werenae *that* daft!

A PAIR O' PURPLE BREEKS

Hill's Trust School - number 20 on the 1995 Govan Heritage Trail - was opened in 1899. Equally built to last was my own Alma Mater, the nearby Greenfield School which opened for business in 1902. Now well-known as the school attended by best-selling author, Christine Marion Fraser, Greenfield holds an affectionate place in the hearts of thousands of its former pupils the world over.

The same could be said for Fairfield School (1875), Harmony Row (1883), Hill's Trust (1899), and Elderpark School (also 1899).

The form of education was standard throughout all these Govan Parish School Board establishments. That being so, my own memories will doubtless strike a chord in the minds of other Glaswegians, in addition to providing background information for Govan Heritage Trail travellers. So let's take a step back in time to my schooldays in the nineteen thirties during the years of the Depression in Glasgow's Govan...

As with children worldwide, schooldays formed a major part not only of my life in the distant past, but also of my memories nowadays in old age...

The school to which I went was somewhat euphemistically called 'GREENFIELD.' Initially, the name may have been appropriate, but at this distance in time, who knows? All I can say with any degree of certainty is that by the time my cronies, wee brother and myself entered its sacred halls of learning in the 1930's, there was neither anything green not even the smallest patch of land resembling a field within spitting distance of my Alma Mater. But, no! I tell a lie!

There was a parody of a tree which some visiting 'Toon Cooncillor' had once upon a time and in an excess of civic pride planted centre-stage of our concrete playground. This 'tree' which grew stark, bare and soot-laden, no matter the season of the year, was protected by a circle of ornate wrought-iron, the latter acting as a magnet for the heads of generations of Mixed Infants. And by the time my pal Lizzie and I were big girls in the top Qualifying Class, we were quite adept at extricating squealing Mixed Infants whose head had somehow got well and truly stuck through the bars of the fence.

Of course, by then we were sufficiently street-wise to know better than to try to enlist the help of the school Janitor, otherwise known as 'Daft Dunkie' or the Janny.

Had we in fact had the temerity to interrupt the everlasting 'tea-break' of this uniformed and august official then he himself would in turn have reported to a higher authority not only the unfortunate heid-stuck-in-railings Mixed Infant, but also the names of his or her would-be saviours.

And once reported to the 'Heidie' for that, or any other equally heinous misdemeanour, then we would all have got a 'doubler' from Miss Martin's expertly wielded Lochgelly belt. Rumour had it that this caring Infants Mistress, this guardian of young and impressionable minds, actually pickled the instrument of torture in vinegar each night in order to give the three-tongued belt added strength! Of course, as the lowest form of animal or educational life, we had no way of knowing the truth or otherwise of this legend. But one thing was certain - it made us wary of bringing down on our heads - or rather, on our callused, chilblained hands - the wrath of this redoubtable teacher.

Miss Martin, who always wore a dun-coloured smock, in the pocket of which she kept the ever-ready Lochgelly, had yet another talent besides that of Mistress of Torture. She was an enthusiastic, if somewhat unskilled, pianist and what she lacked in finesse of technique, she more than compensated for in her over-zealous use of the loud pedal.

Each morning, on the stroke of nine o'clock, the Janny would appear on the top step at the entrance to the school. In his hands, he carried an enormous brass bell; the peals of which would have awakened the dead, even as far away as Craigton Cemetery.

Terrified as we were of the Janny with his direct line of communication not only to Miss Martin, but also to the 'Heidie' himself, the Janny had only to raise the bell, for us all to assemble at once in a flurry of excitement into soldier-straight lines. Then, on a shouted word of command, and the first sound of piano-notes of military-style music issuing from the central hall, we all but goose-stepped our way, tackety boots and all, into yet another day at Greenfield School.

28

Once inside, we had to march around the perimeter of the hall and heaven alone help any child who over-stepped the thick white line which the Janny, in an excess of zeal as a young man, had painted to indicate the sacred no-child's land beyond.

And as we marched, heads held high, arms swinging, eyes front, it is true that we sometimes did live rather dangerously in trying to sneak a sideways glance at our very own concert pianist! I can see her yet, ram-rod straight, perched atop a velvet-covered piano-stool, the mahogany handles of which would have supported an ocean-going liner, never mind Miss Martin and her enormous bosom; and her fish-cold eyes pinned, not on the piano, but instead ever on the alert for any recalcitrant child. One strongly-shod foot was pressed hard on the loud pedal, her bony fingers crashing down on the ivories, and all the while, with each movement of her head, there would be a scattering of steel hair-pins as they struggled to free the prison of her tightly-wound, regulation school-ma'am bun.

Once safely arrived in our own classroom, and according to our place in the scheme of things, we either shambled into the bottom row or else marched proudly to the middle or even triumphantly to the top step of the tiered classroom. And when once seated at the robust wooden desks with their attached seats, we sat bolt upright, arms folded in the standard approved manner, and waited for the day's educational process to begin. It is true to say, that ever-terrified of getting the belt, we hung on teacher's every word, chanted our 'Times Tables', sang out our spelling rules, and regurgitated reams of the most sick-making poetry, not to mention yards of Proverbs and endless chapters from the 'Guid Book.' Then too at the drop of a hat, we could churn out lists of historic dates, British rivers, towns and industries; could point out with pride the vast areas of the world in pink which designated the noble British Empire; and could, with the greatest ease, write an essay on 'The Journey of a Penny.'

I had first enrolled as a five-year-old 'Mixed Infant' at Greenfield School in 1933. By the age of eleven when I graduated to Govan High School, in common with the majority of my chums, I was already something of an expert at Biblical history and quotations, spelling, the writing of essays and the finer points of grammatical usage. I could

29

pick out predicate, subject, verb and object with the ease of an Honours Graduate in English and even the odd Iambic Pentameter was not beyond me. That was the good news!

The bad news was that I loathed, with every fibre of my being, Mental Arithmetic. The weekly Friday morning tests in this particular subject were, for me, not so much mental arithmetic, but rather more of a form of mental torture!

There was hardly a Friday dawned but what I tried - usually unsuccessfully - to persuade Mammy that I was about to be plunged into the throes of yet another bilious attack. As a child, I was very prone to this nauseating condition, but despite my best efforts at 'pretend' boaking and retching, nevertheless I just could not manage to programme the attacks to fit my own desired timetable.

Even worse, with her in-built radar, Mammy could spot a phoney at a mile off! The days when I saw my dear Mother approaching my bed with a vinegar-rag for my aching head and a sick-bowl at the ready for my eventual outpourings, were the times I knew that she believed me. Yes! This was the real thing ... but sadly, never, ever on a Friday!

Another pet hate of mine at school was Music. No, not classical pieces, nor even the already well-loved airs of Scotland. What I refer to were those accursed Tonic Sol-fa books and accompanying Chart, the latter invariably prodded at frequent intervals with a stout wooden pointer expertly wielded by our over-enthusiastic teacher.

And each time that the pointer crashed down on my desk, my heart would sink to my boots for I knew that it would be my turn to "do the next bit, Jenny McCracken." Despite my best efforts, I just could not get to grips with the eternal mysteries of the Tonic Sol-fa system. Then, with my rubbishy answer, in stark contrast to my known skill in English subjects, no doubt my teacher thought I was trying to 'come the eejit'. The end result was always the same ... another 'doubler' from that well-used Lochgelly belt! So much for the charms of music!

If I hated Friday mornings, the opposite was the case as far as the last afternoon of the school week was concerned. It was a magical time, especially for avid readers like myself. Each Friday afternoon was when our teacher was required by the School Board, and for all I know, even the very law of the land, to tot up on her Class-Register the statistics as to attendances, absences and suspected truancy.

To complete this complicated process, the poor woman needed peace, quiet and a temporary respite from the demands of close on fifty young children. So it was that she had devised a master-plan for her own salvation ... she allowed us to 'bring in books' with which to occupy us. Well! It was so quiet in our pseudo-monastic reading-room on those occasions, that even the turning of a page too noisily was rewarded with a bitter look from Miss McMaster, especially if her calculations were going badly.

However, once the completed document had been given into the care of the 'quietest boy or girl in the class', and thus sent on its way to a higher authority, then and only then would our teacher relax. Whatever trauma the week may have held was over, and the rest of the afternoon was given over to the delights of having our teacher read to us a few chapters from a 'good book.'

The only other occasions when we would be read to in this soothing, educational, and highly enjoyable way would be on Sewing Days. At these times, the boys having been marched off to another classroom, there to try a spot of Handwork, we girls had peace to don our lap-bags without ribald comments. Then, suitably attired, we settled down to sew our patchwork samples, knit our never-ending scarves and socks, all the while listening to the careful pronunciation and tortured vowels of a 'good reader.'

This is perhaps an appropriate point at which to conclude my memories of Primary Schooldays. Mention of sewing and knitting, other areas in which I most definitely lacked prowess, calls up vivid mental pictures of a mis-matched pair of socks, a pom-pom which fell apart at a touch, a lap-bag, designed to house knitting, the sides of which I had inadvertently stitched up, thus negating the object of the exercise!

But surely the greatest sewing-disaster of my schooldays - the very thought of it, even sixty-one years later, still brings a blush to my withered cheeks - was a hideous pair of breeks - purple, embroidered and pocketed knickers, the elastic of which snapped at the first wearing!

THERR'S A MAN IN THE LOBBY

The myriad sights, sounds, tastes and smells of Govan are inextricably linked in my memory and would fill an entire book on their own. And obviously they were not, nor ever could be, confined to one calendar year alone.

However, having said that, by the year 1933 I had reached the age of five years old and, as detailed in the previous chapter, was by then a pupil at Greenfield Primary School. With the excellent thorough grounding and superb teaching of a Scottish Parish School Board education quickly getting into first-gear in my young life, I was already becoming more mentally alert and much more aware of the fascinating facets of life all around me. 1933 was also the year in which I learnt many of the eternal truths of life.

To me, in the dawn of my new awareness, there seemed to be a cast of thousands, interesting characters one and all, who either were permanent fixtures, flitted through my life, or played out their parts on the fringes of my childhood.

There were my beloved and loving parents; my grandparents, one set of whom had originally eloped from Ireland in the face of fierce family opposition to a 'mixed' marriage in which, in the attitudes of the day, it was taboo to marry a social inferior; Govan's kindly but strangely named Doctor Dagg, whom with childish glee, I mentally christened Doctor Jag. However, in those dim and distant days, children were required only to be seen, not heard, so I kept my literary witticisms to myself. There was the 'Nit Nurse' at school who hunted for head-lice with all the zeal of a gold-miner in search of treasure; the Heid Bummers at school who included our teachers, the Jannie or caretaker and of course the Headmaster, otherwise known as the 'Heidie.' There was the briquette man; the knife-grinder, the... Hold on! Let us now take a step back in time and allow ourselves a closer look at some of these characters, now gone for ever, but the memory of whom will be ever fresh in my mind.

Each district of Glasgow had its own assortment of characters, each with his or her own distinctive appearance, sound and it must be said, smell. Mention of 'smell' leads me first of all to think of 'Stinky Malinky' the fish-wife, whose fragrance on the summer air could be sniffed at a mile off! A wraith of a woman, she nevertheless had the strength of ten, as clothed in her long skirt, sack-cloth apron and her man's cloth bunnet, she trundled her barrow-load of fish from one street to the next. In addition to her distinctive odour, she had a trademark sound, which issued from the bugle she wore slung around her neck. When she was desperate to drum up some much-needed business, she would raise her bugle aloft an 'gie it laldy'.

The Briquette Man was another kenspeckle figure in our streets. A wee bauchle of a man, with his bandy legs and tartan bunnet rammed low on his forehead, he could hardly be seen from behind his enormous barra. He could, however be heard! His leather-lunged voice would bawl out a warning to all and sundry:

"COAL BRIQUETTES! CO-AL BRIQUETTES! Youse'll a' be cauld if you forget. Sae come and buy ma CO-AL BRIQUETTES."

On the days when he wasn't feeling quite so prophetic, but perhaps rather more desperate to make a sale, and in rather more of a literary turn of mind, he would then bawl out his famous rhyming couplet:

"Briquettes! Briquettes! Tuppence a dozen!
Cheapest briquettes in the hale o' Govan!"

On still other days when trade was really slack, he would augment the sound of his voice. On these occasions he would all but sing the poetry of his words to the accompaniment of a wooden rattle which he wheeched around with gusto and a certain degree of expertise. In answer to his serenade, windows would be screeched open in tenement buildings and canny housewives would have a 'hing-oot' the window as they shouted out their esteemed orders, at the same time as engaging in a bit of Glaswegian repartee.

"Heh, Sandy! A coupla dozen'll dae me fine the day. But mind noo, Ah'm for nane o' yer chipped wans. Ma siller's every bit as guid as yer Fancy Wumman roon the corner in Elderpark Street!"

The Glasgow streets of my childhood rang with such repartee and did much to educate me in the ways of life ... even though I never did find out exactly what 'A Fancy Wumman' looked like, and believe me, that was not for the want of trying!

Other kenspeckle figures included Moanin' Minnie, the Rag-Woman, with a sack on her back, money in her apron pocket and steel in her heart when it came to wheeling and dealing; Onion Johnny with his wares and what also appeared to be all his worldly goods balanced precariously on his bicycle; Leerie the Lamplighter - a real decent wee man, with his crooked, bandy shanks and long pole; the Rag-Man with balloons tied to his cart; the Sweep who wandered the streets with his soot-laden brushes; humphy-backet wee Erchie who trundled his wheel in his ongoing search for knives to grind; the Salvation Army with their infectious enthusiasm and their marvellous, rousing music with which they hoped to win, keep and save souls for Jesus.

Then there was Big Malkie, with his fruit barra and his promise of dietary delights. He too had something of a literary turn of mind with his oft-quoted:

"Honey Perrs! Honey Perrs! Buy them noo for up yer sterrs." Another of his poetical gems, whose aim was to encourage the audience to buy his bananas, also played a somewhat raucous part in the scheme of things:

"BANANAS! BANANAS! Buy them noo or else ye'll cry,
When ye see the wee bananas passin' by!"

Nor must we forget the Midden Men, who with candle-lamps stuck in the front of their caps, disturbed the hours of darkness with their night-soil vehicles; and the Milkmen who rattled steel churns and cans in the early morning. These were the sounds of my childhood, with many others such as the clink of a few coppers as they hit the back-courts to encourage the Street Entertainers, and always like a Greek chorus, the eternal cry:

"Mammy! Mammy! Fling us doon a jeelie-piece! Gonnae dae it, Mammy? Ah'm fair stervin' o' hunger! Uch, go on, Mammy!"

Such were the sounds that made up the symphony that was not only Govan but also many other parts of the City of Glasgow in the 1920's and 1930's.

Less voluble, but still an integral part of the scene were the Tarrie-biler and Watter-cert men, the Tally-man, otherwise known as the Ticky-man; the bottle-clinking Bleach-man; and Mr. Grey, the wee

Insurance-man, a figure of importance and authority with his gaffer's bowler hat, his umbrella and the document-case, his badge of office.

In later years, and it must be admitted that memory blurs as to exactly when these other characters first appeared on the Govan scene, we had regular visitations from the Kleen-eezee man with his cargo of mops and brushes; the Lemonade-man with his slogan:

"STILL-ADE makes thirst a joy."

And to swell even further the ranks there was the Encyclopaedia would-be salesman with his hard-luck tales of his own impoverished student days and his exorbitant promises of education, enlightenment and a glowing future for ragged, slum weans who would not know what a Hall of Learning looked like, even had they met it in their porridge!

One particular favourite of mine was Notteriani, the Ice-cream man with his bottle of red fluid for that most delicious of treats, a MacCallum poky-hat; the Hoover Salesmen with their bags of rubbish at the ready, these to be thrown down on previously clean floors for an instant demonstration; and the Newspaper-subscription-men with their many fascinating and often far-fetched inducements to buy.

Pleasant sounds included those of the ships' sirens coming from the river; the cries of street traders and back-court entertainers and perhaps best of all, when times were better and men were again employed in the shipyards, the sound of the shipyard horns summoning men to their guid work, not forgetting the quarter-to-one "bummer", which blew loudly to indicate that dinnertime was over and that work was about to re-start at one o'clock precisely.

Smells from my childhood included the stench from the River Clyde, the stink from the back-court middens, the delightful aroma of ham and lentil soup, and of course, the heady whiff of boiling tar which emanated from the Tarry-Biler which cruised around our streets. Mention of the Tarry-Biler evokes a dozen different mental pictures and I could quite happily devote an entire chapter to this topic alone. However, all the weans of my generation who skipped along in the wake of a Tarry-Biler, with the resultant skelpit-letherin' from Mammy on later trailing globules of melting tar over a clean floor, will have their own clear-cut memories. One particular facet I would mention is that in addition to the hordes of weans, the Tarry-Biler men also had to cope with an assortment of somewhat distraught women with children happed up in plaid shawls. Clutching these bairns to the bosom, these mothers marched along as close to the machine with its cauldron of boiling tar as they dared. This was in the fond belief that the auld wives' tale might have a measure of truth in it and if so, then the fumes of boiling tar would cure their offspring of that most loathsome of diseases, namely the whooping-cough.

Another powerful and evocative smell was that encountered in the Subway, the latter being the name used by all Glaswegians for the Underground, which was a very cheap and useful mode of public transport.

One sight which may well have baffled any stranger to our streets was that of a square piece of card with a set of initials printed on it which was displayed in the window of many a tenement. To the initiated, this indicated that the housewife wished her coalman to call and deliver some urgently-required bags of coal.

Simple games were an integral part of a Thirties childhood, with such delights as Kick-the-can, Leavo, Hide-and-seek, skipping-ropes, peever, whips and peeries, moshie, marbles, otherwise known as bools or jauries, girds and cleeks, bogies, and that everlasting favourite, scraps, with sets of heavenly angels being my own particular favourites. If for some reason, things were not going well with any game, or perhaps when Mammy shouted to us to come in for dinner, tea or bedtime, then the shout would go up;

"The gemme's a bogey, the gemme's a bogey."

Thereupon, our pals would join in the chorus;

"The gemme's a bogey. Therr's a man in the lobby."

For all I know the man may still be 'in the lobby' ... I was never brave enough to go and find out!

FOOTNOTE: In some parts of England, notably in Stoke-on-Trent, the word 'lobby' is used to indicate a kind of soup or stew. However, for the sake of clarity, it should be pointed out that in Glesga parlance, a 'lobby' is an entry or passageway.

A SQUEAKY PULLEY

In the closely-packed tenement buildings, noises-off were a permanent feature of our lives. One which stands out vividly was the blood-curdling screeching of a squeaky pulley. A pulley was a wooden-frame drying rack fitted with wheels which enabled it to be hoisted up to the ceiling. Since every home had one and given that some neighbours were more 'eechy-ochy' in caring for the comfort of others, this meant that many a family row ensued. Was it Daddy's turn to go upstairs and read the riot act with that 'clarty wee messin' who would lie all day in her scratcher rather than take the trouble to oil the wheels of her pulley? Or would it be Mammy's turn this time to issue a warning? And if so, would the broom handle banged against the ceiling be sufficient reminder to the 'durty midden' and her 'wee nyaff o' a man?'

Somehow, the grating sound of a squeaky pulley was enough to drive the most solid citizen berserk! And when it was not actually in full flight, as it were, it was almost as nerve-wracking to the captive audience to sit poised, listening intently, and just waiting for the next diabolical screech.

Mind you, it was every bit as bad with Big Erchie's boots. Big Erchie was the clarty wee midden's apology for a man and never a night but what he came home, usually 'legless' frae drink, and dropped one boot from a great height, then seemingly to disappear off the face of the earth, before finally - and blissfully to the ears of his waiting and impatient audience in the single-end below - letting go of the second boot.

Other noises-off included screaming weans, mewling cats, fighting dugs, drunken revellers, warring husbands and wives, scrabbling rats in the back-court middens, not to mention the night-soil men with their cap-lanterns, and the ongoing rushing of many waters from the stair-heid cludgie. And let us not forget the squeaking of casement windows, a sound that to me, was worse than the times that Miss McMaster would scrape her fingernails along the surface of the blackboard. And of course, it must be admitted that we weans also contributed much to the ongoing and horrendous cacophony of tenement life.

Any time that our back-court games became over-rumbustious, we weans had to keep a weather-eye open for old Mr. Rafferty up on the third floor of our tenement. The first sign that he was annoyed at our racket would be the screeching of his casement window as he decided to enter the fray, albeit from a distance. "Will youse weans stop that bloody racket! Ah'm trying for tae get a decent bit doss in ma ain bed!"

Some of the older boys who prided themselves on their prowess at running, would sometimes reply with such pleasantries as: "Uch awa' and bile yer heid, Rafferty. Better still, get yersell back tae yer Emerald Isle that ye're aye yappin' on aboot."

"Will youse weans stop that bloody racket"

Such an exchange invariably ended in one way. Risking life and arthritic limb, the crotchety auld man, who I now realise, to my shame, wanted only a spot of peace in the Autumn of his life, would lean even further out over the rotting window-sill. Between the physical effort and his by-now uncontrollable rage, he would be purple in the face.

"Cheeky wee brats that youse are. Ah'll tell yer Mammies, so Ah will! Then it'll be a belt aroon the lug-hole or a guid skelpit letherin' for every last one o' youse."

If anything, such threats shouted in the strange mixture of an Irish brogue and the glottal stops of an adopted Glesga accent, served only to goad we disruptive weans to further heights of bravado. Then the mottled face would disappear, to be followed a few seconds later by the cascading contents of a bucketful of cold water. Thanks to long practice, we weans were pretty adept at side-stepping such an expected waterfall.

But heaven help any unsuspecting housewife or by-passing itinerant back-court songster, even then just getting into his stride with the opening bars of 'THE OLD RUGGED CROSS.' There was hardly a single day passed in the Thirties but what I heard at least one rendering of 'THE OLD RUGGED CROSS.' Our back-court in Langlands Road was a mecca for the hordes of wandering street Entertainers.

In the main, these were unemployed men, each dressed in uniform of cheap, thin suit, long white tasselled scarf, and a flat cloth bunnet. Invariably, their hands would be thrust deep into their pockets, their shoulders hunched and the bunnets pulled low, as if not only to hide the misery in sunken eyes from their audience, but also to blot out the hell of their surroundings. From the haven of lowered eyes could be seen no rat-infested back-court, already teeming with scavenging cats; no fighting dogs, nor even no skimpily-clad, nit-ridden, nose-running weans.

Other unemployed men who tried to keep mind, body, soul, and family together in the hellish days of the Depression, would do a spoon-and-dance routine; go round with the velvet collecting bag for the hurdy-gurdy man with his monkey, itself better dressed than any bairn in the whole of Govan; or play on a mouth-organ the emotive and highly appropriate tune: "KEEP RIGHT ON TO THE END OF THE ROAD."

Poor, hungered, tortured souls that they were, I have often wondered what the end of their particular road turned out to be!

FAIR REEKIN' O' VINEGAR!

Mammy, in common with every other canny Scottish housewife of her time, seemed to have a ready, home-made cure for almost every ailment known to man and to medical science.

A sore throat? Nae problem! An old woollen sock filled with salt, heated at the kitchen-range and wrapped around the throat would very soon give some easement. However, should that fail, then a more expensive cure was called for ... namely that of butter-balls. One simply rolled a few pieces of specially bought-in butter in a dish of sugar and then let the wean chomp its way through that little lot.

Also, I seem to remember that, more of a preventative than any-thing else, we weans used to wear round our necks, on a piece of grubby string, a circular object rather like a modern-day 'polo-mint'. This had been impregnated with iodine and as it hung negligently between one's upper chest and the rim of one's liberty-bodice, it was supposed to ward off 'flu-germs, assorted lurgae and for all I know, the Evil Eye itself!

Then of course, there were the health-giving properties of sheets of brown paper, home-made poultices, cold tea, sliced raw onions, camphorated-oil, Gregory's Mixture and vinegar rags ... to mention but a few.

Mention of the last-named item opens up a whole vast area. Vinegar was used not only to calm the fevered-brow in the throes of a sick-headache; it also had uses as a cleaning-agent in the sponging of school gym-slips ... not to mention its use as a final rinse which, hopefully, would add new and exciting highlights to my dull-as-ditch-water, moosey-broon hair.

One way and another, I often felt that, given the vast amount of vinegar-fumes wafting about my person at any given moment, I must have wandered around Govan smelling like a chip-shop on a busy Saturday nicht!

Yes! Mammy with a cure for everything from a bilious attack to whooping-cough, when a wee sniff o' the itinerant 'tarry-biler' would work its magic, was a walking Sick People's Dispensary. The tragedy

40

is that when her own turn came and an accident resulted in her contracting Tetanus, it would have taken rather more than a wee dab o' vinegar to save the 'pinkie' of her right hand from amputation.

The strange, inexplicable thing, too, is that Mammy's freak accident and its horrific aftermath, had been 'foretold' many years before! However, the full story of that weird episode must await a future volume of my wee Glasgow reminiscences.

Meantime, sufficient for this chapter to say - whatever ailed Telfie or myself as children - Mammy was as knowledgeable as any Panel Doctor, Nit-Nurse or any other Medical Luminary!

Mammy had a cure for everything

WAITING FOR THE FEVER VAN

Mammy closed the door behind the Doctor and then stood with her forehead pressed against the rough wood of the lintel. With shoulders bent, she clutched on to the door knob and the knuckles of both hands showed white.

As she stared down at her bunched fists, it was as if all the concentration of which she was then capable was pinpointed on those fists which stored her fears, her emotions, and all the pent-up anxiety of the past few hours.

At a sound from the bed, Mammy's back stiffened. She prised her fingers from the door-knob and as if summoning all her inner strength, turned back to face the room and all that it held for her.

From where I sat on the fender-stool, I looked up and frowned at what I saw in Mammy's eyes. It was a long time since I had seen Mammy give way to emotion. In fact, not since that terrible night when I had dragged a screaming and terrified wee Telfie over the waste-ground short-cut and we had both been in grave danger of assault from a drunken lout. At the memory of that hellish night, I shook my head as if to free myself of the still-vivid mental pictures.

The sudden movement caused Mammy to be aware of me. At once, she screwed up a corner of her coarse apron and dabbed at her eyes and cheeks. That done, she pinned a travesty of a smile to her face and said,

"Jenny! Don't just sit therr! Get the kettle on."

I rose to my feet and made to go towards the sink. As I did so, Mammy kept on speaking, muttering to herself, and almost as if seeking comfort of some sort from the sound of her own voice.

"Aye, Jenny. A wee cuppa tea! That's whit we need. And onywey, it'll help pass the time. While we're waiting, like."

I was completely at a loss to know what was happening or even have an inkling as to what on earth we could possibly be awaiting. I beetled my brows and then over the sound of Telfie's laboured breathing, I ventured to ask, "Waiting, did ye say, Mammy? But whit are we waitin' for? The Ticky-man was here last week. And it's no' even the richt day for the wee Insurance man, wi' his bowler, his umbrella and his swanky attaché-case. So, whit ur we waitin' aboot for? Ah don't get it, Mammy."

Mammy's eyes again filled with tears

At this innocent question, Mammy's eyes again filled up with tears and it was clear that she had to struggle to regain her composure. When she could at last trust herself to speak, the words came out in the form of a reprimand for me.

"Ye don't get it! Cheeky wee midden, that ye are .... I'll tell ye whit ye'll get in a meenit - ma hand aff yer jaw, that's whit ye'll get."

I opened my mouth to protest but Mammy was too quick for me.

"Lissen, Jenny! Ah'll mak a pot o' tea. Jist you run next door tae Grannie's. She'll hae saw the Doctor in the close onywey, and tell her tae come ben the hoose for a meenit."

No sooner had Granny been summoned and escorted into our home, than Mammy, with a cry like that of a wounded animal, collapsed into the nearest chair. She lowered her head onto her hands and sat there, shoulders heaving, her whole body racked with misery.

Then looking up at the older woman, she stretched out her hands as if in supplication and said,

"Oh, Granny, Granny! Why does the Guid Lord allow such suffering. It's wee Telfie! The Doctor, Doctor Dagg - he said .... he said .... they'll no' be long. The men, they should be here ony minute. Oh, Granny, whit am Ah gonnae dae? Puir wee Telfie, he's a wee innycent lamb, disnae deserve tae suffer."

At these words, Granny threw me a meaning look, as if not only did she blame me for all Telfie's problems, she felt it would have been less of a trauma all round had I myself been the victim of the Guid Lord's displeasure.

Anxious to escape, I busied myself in pouring out two enamel mugs of tea. Then as I set them down on the waxcloth cover, some of the tea slopped over. I gasped! But for once both Mammy and Granny were too occupied with their own thoughts to trouble about my slovenly habits. Even so, old habits die hard, so just to be on the safe side, I extracted a rag from my knicker-pocket and proceeded to mop up the surplus liquid.

As the two women sipped at their tea, the only sounds in the room were the ticking of the clock, the rattle of spent coals, the drip, drip, dripping of the gooseneck tap, and the strangled sound of heavy, laboured breathing coming from a fitfully-sleeping Telfie.

Granny McGuinness was the first to speak and somehow, the words seemed to be forced out of her,

"Poor darlin' Telfie! He's that wee! Nuchin' much tae fecht back wi', has he?"

Mammy nodded, opened her mouth to speak and eventually managed to say, "Aye, puir wee lamb. And Doctor Dagg says, nae doubt aboot it, the wee fella's got the fever."

At these words, I brightened and breenged ram-stam into the conversation. "Fever, did ye say, Mammy? Uch, forget it! That's nuchin! Ma pal, Lizzie, had the fever. A week in bed, buckets o' ice-cream, plenty o' ginger for tae drink. She had a rerr time. Back tae schule, nae bother at a'."

With a great air of deliberation, Mammy laid down on the table the chipped enamel mug, studied me as if I wisnae quite the full twenty-shillins in the pound, then said slowly and carefully, "Aye, Jenny hen, ye're richt. Lizzie had it. But therr's wan thing ye don't seem tae understaun .... it was jist an ordinary fever yer pal had. Whit Telfie has is the Daddy o' them a' .... It's something called the Scarlet Fever. And therr's a big difference, darlin'. Aye!" and here Mammy sighed deeply, "A muckle great difference, Jenny hen."

It seemed as if Granny was about to give me a lecture on the horrors of Scarlet Fever, when a sudden banging at the door caused all three of us to jump in alarm. Old Granny was the first to recover, and arthritic limbs or no', she seemed to bound to the door, which she opened with a single deft movement.

There on the doorstep stood two men, strangers. At the sight of them, Mammy gasped. Between them they were carrying two long poles wrapped around with canvas. No word was spoken but they pushed the door wide and Granny stood back to let them enter the room.

I noticed that one man had a blanket draped over his arm. The brilliant colour of the wool stood out in sharp contrast to the dark of his uniformed sleeve. While the other man exchanged a few whispered words with Mammy, the man with the blanket approached the bed and its tiny occupant.

By the bedside, he stood looking down at the restless child, puir wee Telfie, whose right arm was thrown back on the pillow, while his other hand, clenched and damp, was stuffed halfway into his mouth.

The man turned away from the bed, and on seeing me crouched low on the fender stool, he threw me a brief nod and a kindly smile which reached his eyes. Then turning his attention to his colleague, he said,

"It's no' a stretcher job this, Jimmy! We'll manage up jist fine wi' the blanket alone. The puir wee mite wid be lost, like a pea on a clooty-dumplin', if we wis for tae put him on the stretcher."

At these emotive words, Mammy let out a strangled cry. Meanwhile, the ambulance-man turned back to the bed, bent down and with careful movements, pulled away the patchwork quilt.

There lay Telfie, his small body encased in his best jumble-sale sleeping-suit, the scruffy rabbit on the pocket already limp and saturated with sweat.

With great care and tenderness, the ambulance-man lifted Telfie. When all that could be seen of the puir wee mite was the mop of damp curls, Mammy stretched out her hand for one last fond touch. At a nod from the man holding Telfie, the other man opened the door and stood with his hand on the brass-knob.

Even I, young though I was, knew that there was nothing more to be done, nothing further to be said. Although I did privately wonder what had happened to Telfie's usual luck, the never-failing good fortune of the universally-adored "jammy wee bassa".

CLOOTIE DUMPLIN'

Clootie Dumplin' was my favourite food and the delicious aroma of the treacle, currants and raisins was enough to set the mouth watering. 'Clootie Dumplin' gets its name from the fact of its being boiled or steamed when wrapped securely in a scalded cloth. Mammy would tie the four corners of the cloth tightly together, then slip a wooden spoon under the knots before lowering the pudding into a pot of boiling water. Once cooked, she would unwrap the steaming delicacy and set it by the fire to harden and hopefully, get a nice skin on it.

In our home at least, 'Clootie Dumplins' were made only on very special occasions, all of which of course, added to their attraction. And to add further to the excitement, it was the normal Scottish custom to wrap up, in paper, 'favours' and slip these deep inside the pudding. I suppose that nowadays such a ploy would be frowned upon by the Health and Safety moguls. Whatever of that, I never once heard of any child choking over a 'favour' ... I suppose we were all too busy hunting feverishly through our portion of pudding to be caught unawares!

And what exactly were these 'favours?' As I recall, there were four varieties. One was a nail-sized white China doll; another was a tiny thimble; a third was a button; and the prize of them all ... a silver threepenny bit!

There was even an entire tradition of superstitious beliefs relating to the finding of these small items. For instance, if you unwrapped the paper to discover a button, this meant, if male, that you would be a bachelor; while a thimble predicted a lifetime of spinsterhood for a girl; and perhaps even worse, if a boy should be unlucky enough to get a thimble, or a girl won a bachelor-button, then horror of horror, this indicated a life of penury; a white China doll foretold a life of wedded bliss for either boy or girl; while best of all, the much sought-after silver threepenny piece presaged riches beyond the dreams of avarice!

Usually, if there was enough dumplin' left, this would be reserved for frying in slices the next day. However, if we had escaped Mammy's eagle eye long enough to wade our way through until there was only one tiny piece left, then Mammy would always say in proffering it;

"Tak this last bit, hen. And if ye don't speak while ye're eating it, when ye're a big girl, ye'll be sure tae have either a handsome husband or a thousand-a-year!"

This saying was trotted out every time that the last portion of any delicacy was on offer, be it dumplin', sody scone, hot pancake, Black Bun or whatever. I often wondered if it were merely a ploy on Mammy's part to gain a couple of minutes' peace, as the hopeful one chomped in silence, meanwhile dreaming impossible dreams. After all, who had ever heard of a thousand pounds a year! Surely not even the King in England, doon therr in London, was as rich as that!

Another favourite saying applied to the regular family get-togethers for Sunday high tea. If Mammy had but a limited number of short-bread-pieces available, for instance, then before the Aunties, Uncles, Grandparents and Cousins were due to arrive, there would be a select family conference at which Mammy would say;

"Noo then, youse lot! As far as the shortbreid goes, it'll be a case of faimly haud back!"

Not that the family ever did "haud back" when the famous 'Clootie Dumplin' was on offer ... then it was a case of every man, woman and child for himself! And the golden rule was: you didn't stop eating until your belly was near to burstin'.

Without fail, every year on the first Friday in June, Mammy always made a special celebration 'Clootie Dumplin'. This was the traditional day of the Old Govan Fair, a notable event in Govan's annual calendar. Originally started in the Fifteenth Century, the Fair was revived in 1756, after which, with the foundation of the Govan Weavers, it came into its own. In this way it lasted until the year 1881, before again, fading into the mists of time.

However, it was revived in 1920, so by the time I was old enough to enjoy it, with its parade, floats, fancy costumes and pipe bands, it was yet again in full swing. At the head of the procession was always the decorated Sheep's Head hoisted aloft on a pole. It was many years before I discovered the significance of this ... apparently the Sheep's Head was the emblem of the weavers, an important, influential, and hard-working group of craftsmen in Govan during the nineteenth Century.

Following the Sheep's Head would ride the Govan Fair Queen and her attendants, the Fair Queen resplendent in her traditional purple cloak and crown. Certainly a wonderful sight.

For many years I had the fanciful notion that since I myself had never had the good fortune to be chosen as the Old Govan Fair Queen, then Mammy made the 'Clootie Dumplin' as a sort of consolation prize. Who knows? I may have been right in holding to this theory. At any rate, one thing I do know ... there was great comfort in eating one's way through a mound of good old 'Clootie Dumplin', and ever-hopeful that although I had not won a crown, I might yet gain a 'thruppeny bit.'

It is indeed true that 'hope springeth eternal in the human breast!'

THE GLESGA SENSE O' HUMOUR

Recently, one of my loyal readers, a retired Professor, wrote to me from Eastern Canada where he now lives. In Manuel's case, his tenement home in Glasgow had been in the Gorbals district. There in a two-room-and-kitchen flat, he spent his boyhood-days with his loving parents and their 'steps-n-stairs' eight other children. From such an environment, the learned Professor Manuel Linden grew up believing that what matters most in life is people.

His kind, thought-provoking letter and emotive poem: "Ode to Human Dignity", sent my own memories yet again racing back down the years to recall the many people I had known in the dark days of the Glasgow Depression. Some of them I knew well, others I had met but briefly on life's journey, while still others, I had only heard about. And yet, the strange thing is that they all not only left an indelible impression on my mind, they also taught me something of value in my education for life.

For instance, there was Hannah, a poor trauchled old-before-her-time woman, with a drunken husband and four unemployed sons. In my early-morning walks with Daddy down to Auld Mac's Restaurant, where, before setting off for school, I would help prepare the vegetables for the day's cauldron of Scotch broth, we would often meet Hannah.

"Uch, it's yersell, Hughie!" she would say. "Just see ye tim plenty o' lentils intae the soup the day! Yon last lot was gey skimpy!"

At once ready for the usual Glasgow repartee, Daddy would then give as good as he got, and the exchange inevitably ended in good hearty belly-laughs all round, with as ever, Hannah having the last word:

"Aye, Hughie! Just mind whit Ah'm sayin' tae ye. Ye're a lucky man! Ye've got a job! Lissen, son! Whit's aboot ye leavin' that wee wifie o' yours? Ye could come an be ma fancy-man - and keep me in style, eh, no?"

Later on in our travels we would meet up with Postie, perhaps a coalman or two labouring up to tenement top-flats with a burden of coal on bowed-back and on the odd occasion, even Stoorie Sammy on his way home from an all-nighter at the local bakery. And tired, trauchled, overburdened as they were, each and every one had a wonderful ready wit, quick repartee and the indefinable, but very real, 'Glesga sense of humour.' This is something that being inbred, nurtured and well-used by generations of Glaswegians can neither be taught, successfully aped, nor even properly explained. Perhaps the best way to illustrate it is by a specific example ...

I once heard of a waitress in a posh 'silver-service' restaurant (not Mac's Restaurant, I hurry to add!) who had taken the meal-orders for various individual requirements as to such vegetables as peas, carrots or spinach. Later, bearing aloft in grand style a platter of spinach, she approached the seated party of business-men and in strictly aff-the-tap-o'-her heid repartee, demanded to know:

"Richt noo! And whit wan o' youse lot is Popeye!"

It takes a Glaswegian to appreciate such badinage ... which, incidentally was more than did those businessmen! Strangers not only to the Second City of the Empire, but also completely alien as to any understanding of its zany humour, the unhappy would-be spinach eater took umbridge at the girl's extraneous remarks. Other Glaswegians will be appalled to learn that even worse than just going into a 'huff', the black-affrontit diner complained to the Management, who in turn, later sacked the unsuspecting waitress! Rough justice indeed!

The list of people whose lives touched mine in my early formative years is endless. Perhaps this is as good a point as any at which to mention oor Meenister o' the Kirk. I wondered whether or not to include him in the chapter with the other 'high heid yins'. However, since I always thought of him in a class of his own, and since we've been talking of amusing incidents anyway, let's not delay a minute longer in taking a wee keek back in time at that man among men, our very own Reverend gentleman. Yes indeed, another august figure who loomed large in my childhood years was that of the 'Meenister' of our local Kirk. His sermons were of the 'fire and brimstone' variety, but for me, at least, were always considerably lightened by my dear old Granny McCracken, who with bulging sweetie-poke secreted in her handbag, would surreptitiously slip me endless supplies of Mint Imperials, Soor Plooms, or even on rare occasions when she really wanted to shut me up - conversation lozenges!

To this day, in my mind's eye, I can still see our Preacher thumping right heartily at the Pulpit in his earnest desire to emphasise some vital point of Canon Law. In fact, on at least one occasion, the fiery Preacher got so carried away by the fervour of his own oratory that a spar of the oaken Pulpit loosened and flew out like a missile into the body of the Kirk and coursed at high speed for the unsuspecting heads of his captive congregation!

Still, even this was a small price to pay if it meant that as a bonefide member of Saint Gabriel's Sunday School, I was entitled to attend the various 'bun-fights', soirees, Hallowe'en parties, Lantern-Lectures and Sunday School outings to local parks.

The latter events really were dramatic high-spots in our young lives, when almost sick with excitement, and with regulation enamel mug on a string around the neck, we would march to a nearby park, there to sing hymns, say a prayer or two, and then run an assortment of races. Later still we would 'stuff oor turkeys' to near bursting point with cold mutton pies, fern cakes and Empire biscuits, all washed down with copious draughts of 'Ginger', as we Glaswegian weans always referred to Lemonade.

But for all the Meenister's fine words, dramatic perorations, Pulpit-thumping and Bible-bashing, I can honestly say that my true and long-lasting moral values for life were learned, as generations of law-abiding Scots before me, at my dear Mother's knee. She it was who taught me to respect the feelings of others, to give of my best possible efforts in all manner of situations and to own up for my misdeeds, whatever the possible consequences. She impressed on me to be ever-aware that like a pebble flung into the Elder Park Boating Pond, actions, deeds, even words when once launched could not be recalled, but instead caused ever-widening ripples on the Ocean of Life. Certainly a valuable training for responsible adulthood.

A WEE TATE O' GRAVY

While I had an ever-open gub for any 'sweet-bite' which might have been on offer, the same could not be said where my pet hate, Scotch mutton pies, was concerned. The taste, sight and smell of Scotch mutton pies will be with me forever!

Given the fact of Daddy's working in the 'Workman's Restaurant', this meant that any food leftovers became our family's staple diet for that particular week. And yes! you've guessed it ... this meant that more often than not, we dined off Scotch mutton pies.

Now, there are some items of food which can be disguised or even doctored in some ways to present a different appearance, but sadly, the Scotch mutton pie is not one of them. Had it been Daddy's famous home-made little ashet-pies with their delicious layers of flaky pastry, that would have been an entirely different matter! But, as my luck would have it, each day, Daddy's homebaking, a real luxury and highly popular in Govan in the 1930's, always disappeared "faster than snaw aff a dyke." All of which invariably left me sitting with my 'mumper face' on, and ready to do battle with Mammy and with my least favourite food. I can see the scene yet ...

"But, Mammy, Ah'm no' that awfy hungert. Onywey, we had these rotten auld pies yesterday. And the day afore that as weel!"

Mammy turned off the goose-neck tap at the jaw-boax. Then, as she approached the wax-cloth-covered table, she wiped her hands on her heavy duty sack-cloth apron. She put out a placatory hand and ruffled my hair. "Aye! And like as no', ye'll be havin' a Scotch mutton pie the morn as weel, ma wee Jenny, hen!"

When my cries of distress and disgust brought little or no response, I decided to try a different tactic.

"Uch, Mammy! Ah'm ferr scunnert wi' them, so Ah am. In fact, wan mair moothfu' and it'll be enough tae hae me boakin' ma hert up."

"Noo, that's just enough o' that stupit bletherin', Jenny. Eat up yer pie like a guid girl. It'll mak ye big and strong. Ad forbye, while ye're at it, jist you gie a wee bit thought tae thon stervin' children o' China and a' thae ither foreign-like places that the Meenister's aye

52

haverin' on aboot."

Seeing that on this occasion, there was to be no escape, I started crying noisily, at the same time as stabbing with my fork the now stone-cold and unappetising-looking pie. Taking in my tear-begrutten face, Mammy laid a work-worn hand on my cheek. Then, with unseeing eyes, she gazed at a point far removed from the iron bars of the sole window.

"Lissen, Jenny, tell ye whit Ah'll dae. But mind noo, ye've no' tae let on tae yer Faither."

With these words, she whispered in my ear and her message of hope brought a watery smile to my torn face.

Just this once she would heat up a "wee tate o' gravy" and with some leftover mashed-tottie, she would allow me to eat the pie in a fashion that was normally forbidden in the table-manners-conscious McCracken household.

Some time later with gravy and potatoes duly mashed into the rim of the pie, and all thoughts of boakin' and being sick forgotten, I attacked my meal with gusto. As I cleared my plate and finally laid down, with a theatrical flourish, my knife and fork, it was with a sense of achievement and a glow of pride ... the starvin' children of China, India, Africa or any other such far-flung outpost of the Empire would have been proud of me. So also, had they known of my moment of triumph, would have been the Meenister and my Sunday-school teacher, both of whom seemed to spend an inordinate amount of time in worrying about the starving hordes of Asia. Perhaps had they got their act together, and devoted a few more sermons, prayers and bawbees to the unemployed, dispirited and near-starving masses of Govan, they might have had a greater response to their Bible-thumping outpourings.

Anyway, for the moment, in eating up my dinner like a good girl, my own conscience was clear ... I had done my best for the starving children of China. With my temporary halo shining brightly, I took some comfort from my saintly behaviour. One thing was certain ... the next day would bring me face to face again with yet another Scotch mutton pie. And this time, I knew, there would be no "wee tate o' gravy." After all, ye couldnae expect a rerr treat like that every day, now could ye?

LAUNCH-DAYS ON THE CLYDE

Famed worldwide for their shipbuilding skills, the men of Clyde-side surely have led a strange double-life. The craftsmanship, both in building the ships and in fitting them out, was superb. But in creating these sumptuous floating palaces, most of the workmen at day's end had to return to their pathetic, overcrowded and often rat-infested hovels in Govan, Clydebank or Partick - surely a strange contradiction.

The lowest point of the Depression years was when in December, 1931, building on ship no 534 (later to be named the 'QUEEN MARY') was suspended and 3,000 men were laid off work to join the ever-growing numbers of the unemployed. And although almost completed, the abandoned hull all too soon became a pathetic symbol of the nation's Great Depression.

Imagine the excitement, indeed almost the hysteria, when in February, 1934 work re-started on number 534 at John Brown's and men actually *ran* to the shipyard, so desperate were they to begin work again. It had been thanks to the ongoing campaign conducted by Glaswegian David Kirkwood, a Labour Politician, that once again workmen on Clydeside were able to leave the dole-queues and enjoy the dignity and purpose of a day's work well done.

On that September launching day, what could not be seen but what could be felt almost as a tangible presence, was the air of excitement as Queen Mary named the ship which originally Cunard had meant to call 'QUEEN VICTORIA' to be in line with all their other ships such as Lusitania, Carpathia, Ascania, whose names ended in 'ia.' The story goes that with the name of 'Victoria' in mind but not actually mentioned, officials of Cunard contacted King George. They simply made the point that they wished to name ship number 534 after "the most illustrious female Monarch that ever lived." The king replied that his "wife would be delighted!" The rest is history!

To any Clydeside wean, the launching of a ship from one's own local yard was an event worthy of note and one of my fondest memo-ries is of being held aloft on grampa Mac's shoulders, the better to witness a launching at Fairfield's Shipbuilding Yard in Govan.

The launching of a ship from one's own
local yard was an event worthy of note

Mention of Clyde launchings leads me now to a folk-memory often related to me by my Granny Brigton, of a launching which went disastrously wrong. So firmly were the details of this particular disaster implanted in my impressionable young mind that some sixty years later I wrote up a version of the tragedy in my Scottish saga: 'The Kinnons of Candleriggs.'

However, to get the non-fiction tale of the River Clyde's worst-ever shipping disaster, it is necessary to come further back in time with me on a visit to Granny Brigton in her tenement home in Glasgow's East End...

As a child, many a time I sat on Granny Brigton's knee and listened enthralled to her stories which she told in her lovely soft Irish voice.

In those days, I had no way of knowing what was actual historical fact and what owed something, if not all, to granny's vivid imagination. Added to that, in common with her countrywoman, Granny McGuinness, she was at times inclined to be a wee bit 'fey', in that she had on occasion 'seen' into the future. For instance, she had long been 'aware' that a distant cousin who was a fisherman would meet his end by drowning. On the other hand, one of her sons, also a seafarer, who had been born with a caul - a membrane covering his head at birth - would thus be protected from drowning by this talisman of ancient superstition. And any talk of drowning would be enough to trigger off yet another of Granny Brigton's stories.

"Aye," she would say, with a sorrowful nod of her head, "The worst tragedy of drowning I ever heard of was the capsizing of the 'Daphne.' And that at a launching, would ye believe?"

Already wide-eyed and curious, I would believe! Thus suitably encouraged, Granny Brigton would recount her tale.

"It all happened years ago. Even before I came to Glasgow. Let's see ... I came in 1888 ... or was it '87? Never mind! But anyway, I had a good neighbour and she was there, actually there when the tragedy happened! What do you make of that now, Jenny?"

Granny Brigton certainly knew how to get her audience 'hooked'. By that point I would be agog to learn what, when, where and why the catastrophe, whatever it was, had come about.

"Well, it was like this, Jenny. My friend, Theresa, she had a young nephew over from Ireland. He lodged with her, paid his corner, like, and very handy was the extra money. Ye see, he'd got himself a job as a carpenter in Stephen's shipyard, helping to build a fine steamer called the 'Daphne.' A good lad was Desmond and apart from his lodging money, he sent most of his wages to his widowed mother back home in dear old Ireland. Anyway, Theresa was that proud of Desmond, so came the day of the launching of the ship, she herself, a friend and their squad of bairns decided to go to the yard and share in all the fun and excitement of the big day. The shipyard was in Linthouse, near Govan and they had quite a long walk to get there. They set off early in order to get a good vantage point from which to see the launch. As you can imagine, the bairns were all excited and so it didn't need too much prompting to keep them hurrying along the road. Anyway, the sun was shining and it would be a grand day out for the weans. Forbye, Desmond would be aboard, and working below decks to finish off some last-minute carpentry. Yes! even during the naming ceremony and the actual launching, he'd be working. So, he was depending on his Auntie Theresa to tell him all the exciting details later when he'd come home for his tea."

On being asked if there was a huge turnout of folk to see the launching, Granny Brigton said,

"No, 'twas not overcrowded in the yard that day. Don't forget, Jenny, in those days there was hardly a week went past but what there was a launch in one or another of the Clyde shipyards. After all, they were building ships for the whole wide world, and don't you ever forget it, my lass! Anyway, there was maybe a couple of hundred spectators, enough folk to cheer on the 'Daphne' and wish her God-speed. 'Twas a lovely summer's morning in June, or was it July? And as they waited, Theresa blethered to the folk standing round about her. She aye minded of speaking to one middle-aged man who that was that proud, he'd not have called Queen Victoria his Auntie! Seems he had three sons working aboard the 'Daphne' that day. One was a plumber, another a boilerman and his youngest laddie was an apprentice carpenter."

At this point in her story, Granny Brigton would often pause and gaze into a point somewhere above my head. However, another bit of prompting and she would continue.

"Afterwards, Theresa could never forget another near-neighbour, a smiling young woman who had a baby happed up in her shawl and two other wee bairns clinging to her skirts. This young mother too was proud of the fact that her man, unemployed for many a long day, had only a couple of weeks previously started work on the ship. The day of the launching was to have been his day off, but she had persuaded him, against his will, to work the extra shift."

This point of the narrative would warrant yet another silence from Granny before she would finish off in a rush.

"Now then, where was I? Oh aye! About eleven o'clock, or thereabouts, the S.S. 'Daphne', having been duly named, went sliding down the slipway. Just as she entered the River Clyde, that's when it happened. First of all the fine new ship leant over one way, then the other, and then the terrible tragedy ... the 'Daphne' finally capsized altogether. At first the spectators on the shore were numbed into silence and inactivity by the horror they had just witnessed. Aye! a terrible silence there was, according to Theresa. But when the full realisation of the desperate danger into which so many of their loved ones had been plunged, hit their senses, suddenly all was noise and bustle. People started throwing into the water odd pieces of wood and anything at all that would float; small rowing boats put out into the river; other men on the shoreline dived into the murky waters in rescue attempts; and beshawled women reached out and put comforting arms around distraught neighbours and weeping bairns, all of whom, just minutes before, had been cheering the 'Daphne' on her way into the River Clyde. As the ship settled on the bottom of the river, a handful of survivors somehow managed to clamber up on to the hull and there await their eventual rescue. Others had been thrown clear and were clinging to floating pieces of debris. Sadly, poor Desmond was not one of the lucky ones. His body was later recovered and oh! but it was weird. The poor laddie was still holding in his hand the hammer he had been using at the very moment of the disaster. Talk about 'faithful unto Death!' Never was a truer word spoken. And of the eighty or ninety bodies recovered, there were many that had gone to meet their Maker while still clutching in their hands the tools of their trade. 'Twas a strange business altogether on that accursed day."

What of the historical accuracy of Granny Brigton's vivid account of this particular tragedy? The facts are these.

The naming ceremony, launch and capsizing of the 'Daphne' took place on Tuesday, 3rd July, 1883 at the shipyard of Messrs. Alexander Stephen and Company of Linthouse, Glasgow. On that sunny morning, a few hundred spectators, many of whom had relatives aboard, had gathered to watch the launch of the 500 tons steamer. Built for the Glasgow and Londonderry Steam Packet Co. Ltd., the 'Daphne' was intended for use as a carrier of passengers and livestock between Glasgow and various ports in Northern Ireland.

There was something of a last-minute rush to get the ship ready for sailing by the 12th July, which was the start of the Glasgow Fair holidays when the shipyard would be closing for the two-week period. Not only that, the 'Glesga Ferr' was traditionally a time when many Glaswegians of Irish descent returned to the 'Emerald Isle' and would thus provide eager fare-paying passengers for the newly-launched ship.

In view of this race against time, while the naming ceremony and launch were being conducted, below decks, deep in the bowels of the ship, close on 200 workmen were still hard at work.

Up on the main deck and stacked high was a forest of timber planks awaiting the attention of the many carpenters working aboard. When the 'Daphne' capsized, torrents of water poured into the open holds, all of which still lacked essential hatch-covers. In this way, the sinking of the 'Daphne' was exceedingly rapid, as also were the many drowning fatalities.

In all, 124 men lost their lives in the catastrophe and many wives, mothers and children lost not only loved ones but the breadwinner of their families. By the time that the 'Daphne' Disaster Fund had reached a massive £30,000 (of which sum Queen Victoria had contributed a cheque for one hundred pounds) there was many a deserving case in the squalid tenements of Govan, Linthouse and Partick.

By September 5th, 1883, the 'Rothesay Express' was reporting in its columns that "The Executive Committee of the 'Daphne' Fund have resolved to allot the weekly sum of 13/3d (65 pence) to those of the widows of the 'Daphne' sufferers who have been left with children. There are 53 widows in all and the number depending on them is 86. Applications for relief have likewise come from 17 widowed mothers and orphans."

There was a strange sequel to the appalling tragedy. If ever there was such a phenomenon as 'an unlucky ship', then it was surely the S.S. 'Daphne.' When once raised from the river-bed, the 'Daphne' was completely refitted and eventually handed over to her owners. Their first act on taking delivery was, not surprisingly, to re-christen the steamer 'Rose'. But not even that was enough to appease the gods of fortune. On Christmas Day of that very same year of 1883, the ill-fated S.S. 'Rose' sank in Portrush Harbour! In swinging round, the 'Rose' got foul of a ship's anchor and "the anchor going through her bottom, she filled with water and sank at once."

Fortunately, on this occasion although part of the cargo was damaged, there was no loss of life and 'divers were set to work to get the vessel floated as soon as possible.' Thereafter, the 'Rose' went on to sail the Irish Channel between Scotland and Ireland for a number of years and would often pass over the site of her earlier tragedy.

Intensive research for this book has proved that despite a few minor embellishments, it would appear that Granny Brigton did indeed get her historical facts right. Even her story about the magical powers of a caul has a basis of historical data to support her theory. King James VI of Scotland and I of England had been born with such a thin membrane over his face. On 14th March, 1600 he was saved from drowning while returning by ferry to Falkland Palace.

Little wonder then that this superstition has survived through the ages to the extent that seafarers were wont to spend hard-earned money on the purchase of a caul for the sake of such magical protection.

One other thing I learned at Granny Brigton's knee. History was not the dull, moronic chanting of dates, battles and world events as belted into me at Greenfield Primary School and later at Govan High.

History was, and is, about people, real flesh and blood people whose lives are affected, for good or ill, by the times, events and social conditions of the age in which they lived. While I was not aware of it at the time of my growing-up, I now know, some sixty years later, that Granny Brigton taught me well. With her lovely Irish accent, her vivid imagination and her legacy from the Blarney Stone, how could it have been otherwise?

GRANNY - AN IRISH SKIVVY

Grandparents are an important and loving part of any child's up-bringing and in this respect, I was as lucky as most children. One set of my grandparents lived conveniently near in Crossloan Road, which was just around the corner from us. They were usually referred to as Granny and Grampa Govan, Grampa being the resourceful 'Auld Mac' mentioned in a previous chapter.

If the name 'Crossloan Road' should ring a bell for many readers, then that is no surprise, for years later it achieved world-wide fame when best-selling author Christine Marion Fraser, in her splendid Autobiography, 'BLUE ABOVE THE CHIMNEYS' wrote of her childhood room-and-kitchen home in Govan's Crossloan Road.

As for my maternal Grandmother, she lived across the City from us in Glasgow's East End in the Bridgeton district, so naturally she went by the title of 'Granny Brigton.' Somehow, the family always tended to speak of her in hushed, almost reverent tones. As a child, I sensed this and instinctively knew that there was something 'different' about my beloved Granny Brigton.

It was only when I grew up and was privy to adult secrets that I finally learned the truth ... as a young girl in Ireland, Granny had married 'out of her class'. And in those far-off days, with the tightly-drawn lines between the People of Quality upstairs and the Great Unwashed not only below the salt but firmly relegated to the nether regions, there was quite definitely no greater social crime than that of attempting to move out of one's God-given place in the ordained scheme of things!

So, when the young kitchen skivvy had had the temerity not only to fall desperately in love with, but also to elope with the young 'Master' of the grand household in which she herself slaved as the lowest of the low, then from that moment on, as a couple, they were regarded as a race apart! No longer either 'gentlefolk of Quality', nor yet 'Common working folk', they lived in a sort of limbo, and in later years, they were surrounded only by their immediate family.

Over time, they had received too many snubs, insults and unkind, sarcastic comments from all levels of society ever to wish to attempt to mix socially with neighbours, workmates or anyone else outwith their own family.

What must have made their life together even more difficult, if not downright impossible, was the fact that quite apart from the social differences and all the accumulated snobbery from both sides of the great divide, it was also a 'mixed' marriage in so far as religion went.

Granny's home with its crucible of Holy Water, statues of the Virgin and Child, Rosary, paintings of Christ on the Cross, and a print of the famous picture, 'THE LIGHT OF THE WORLD', was a treasure-house for me. As a child brought up as I was in the rather more austere Scottish Episcopal Church, such artifacts were fascinating.

Their 'mixed' marriage would obviously have been under great and constant strain, especially in such a City as Glasgow, a hotbed of seething emotions, and an area long troubled by sectarianism which often led to violence. Having said that, it must be pointed out that the trouble at football matches and in pubs on a Friday or Saturday night was all too often the direct result of drunken confrontations in which real religious beliefs had little or no significance!

The story that sums up for me, at least, the long, deep-seated and cancerous hatred between the two factions is that tale often told - and no doubt embellished with every telling - of a certain Protestant footballer in the 1930's, who, for some reason best known to himself, was playing for Celtic. In the course of a football match in which he had played enthusiastically but perhaps not too well, he had been bawled out by the crowd as being nothing other than 'A bloody Fenian bast..." Later, in attempting to comfort the somewhat dejected and reviled player, a team-mate pointed out that it was really nothing to worry about, since that was what many of the spectators called he himself not just once, but on every conceivable occasion. Kind words of comfort indeed. But what was the reply from the dejected one?

"Aye, that's mibbe richt enough. But the fact remains, let's face it, Paddy ... you *are* a Fenian bast..."

Quite apart from the fascination of her home's religious relics and artifacts, a visit to Granny Brigton was always a great adventure for us weans in the McCracken family. It entailed getting on a yellow tramcar at a stop in Govan Road. We could have caught the same tramcar nearer to our home, but since this would have cost us more money for an additional fare-stage, we were always expected to walk the extra half-mile or so. Story of my life!

A visit to Granny Brigton
was always a great adventure

NO' A CHIP-SHOP IN SIGHT!

By January of 1939, my brother and I were both well into the established routine of our time and generation. This meant a daily attendance at a Parish Board School; Saturday visits to the local 'flea-pit'; and Sunday observance at morning and evening Church services, with for good measure, Sabbath afternoons spent at Sunday-school classes.

Throughout each year, we made it our business to be on hand for as many free 'bun-fights', Lantern Lectures, Band of Hope Soirees, Temperance Teas, and Hallowe'en parties as we could shove, cajole or even fight our way into.

Then too there was the weekly ritual of extended family visiting, when after a slap-up high tea at one or other of the Aunties', there would be endless games of Draughts, Dominoes, or even the occasional card game of 'Stop The Bus.'

By 1939, business at the 'WORKMEN'S RESTAURANT' seemed to be picking up - not that such matters were ever discussed with us - but judging from the fact that our diet was now much more varied, there did not now appear to be quite so many leftover Scotch mutton pies!

In short, everything on our immediate horizon was rosy. Or was it? Unbeknown to us weans, the dark clouds of war were already forming.

Life, as we knew it, was about to change drastically and for ever!

Like many other Glesga weans, we went through the entire process of wartime evacuation not once ... but twice! The story of our first-ever experience of evacuation to Corrie on the lovely Island of Arran, is told in glorious nit-ridden detail in 'TALES OF A GLASGOW CHILDHOOD' (BUSINESSLIKE Publishing 1994).

When I am writing my reminiscences of over sixty years ago, I admit that I often stop in full-flight and with pen poised, ponder the intriguing question,

"Did it really happen that way? Or have I, in using a dollop of poetic licence, perhaps, albeit subconsciously, embroidered the hard facts more than somewhat?"

Well, in the case of our hair-shearing initiation to the lovely Island of Arran, the traumatic event has in fact, been well-documented. Not only does my brother vividly remember the incident, but additional confirmation has come in other surprising, and more roundabout, ways.

Once, when tending my book-stall at a Craft Fayre, a gentleman came up to me, and throwing his arms wide in delight, greeted me like a long-lost relative with the words,

"Jenny Chaplin! At last! I've been searching for you for years!"

No! Not the start of a Barbara Cartland-style romance! It turned out that the said gentleman had read one of my books and he too had been in that self-same, nit-ridden line-up and he wanted to compare notes!

Stranger still, when I was writing this latest book now in your hands, I had a telephone-call right out of the blue from a delightful lady, Maryhill-born and bred, and now living in Stoke-on-Trent. She too had been evacuated to Arran with her school and had also endured the self-same humiliation. Worse still, in her case, once the dire deed of head-shaving had been executed, even then nobody wanted to accept her as an evacuee. Talk about no room at the Inn!

As for our second stab at wartime evacuation in the depths of rural Lanarkshire, with no' a chip-shop in sight, Grampa Mac, in trying to help us hamesick wee Glesga weans get settled, took it upon himself to visit us on a fairly regular footing.

His humanitarian efforts to ease the trauma of our privately-arranged package-deal with the great-granny of a friend, of a friend, on a farm in Coulter, Lanarkshire, had a somewhat bizarre sequel.

Once Telfie and I had bounced back, yet again, to guid auld Glesga toon and were fully recovered from our double-dose of wartime evacuation, we returned to the familiar routine of our life in Govan. But, like I say, there was a strange sequel when Grampa ... but more of that in another chapter!

THE AULD YIN'S WINCHIN!

The year 1940 saw the family re-united in our new 'Cooncil-hoose' in Arklet Road, on the outskirts of Govan. And despite Hitler's bombs which at one point blew out all our windows, we were happy enough in 'oor wee palace' which boasted not only its own bathroom, but also a modern kitchenette, separate bedrooms, a patch of garden for Daddy and even a drying-green for Mammy's washing.

Yes, life was still hard with severe wintry weather, food short-ages, endless queues and all the trauma of war, yet it is the amusing events I remember ... such as the way Mammy would always have to be dragged into our Anderson air-raid shelter, declaring that she'd rather face up to a bomb than encounter a mouse "doon therr in the bowels o' the earth!"

In the middle of World War Two, pages, in fact, whole chapters of history were being enacted, yet the high spot of the decade for me was when Granpa Mac started 'winchin'.

To those unfamiliar with Glesga patter, it should perhaps be explained that 'winchin' can mean anything from going steady with a member of the opposite sex to having a wee bit of a kiss and cuddle in the comparative peace of a tenement's back-close. And of course, 'winchin' was normally associated with the younger element of society and in my experience, had nothing whatsoever to do with auld codgers like Granpa Mac. That day in 1940, I was about to be proved wrong!

As a family, fine well we'd known for a long time that the 'auld yin' was up tae something! Just exactly what that something might be, we then had no way of knowing. So, for a few weeks, we had all kept our dark thoughts and suspicions to ourselves ... or as we used to say in Govan, kept oor geggies, otherwise called our cake-holes, firmly shut.

Secure in the knowledge that truth would out in the end, we merely bided our time. After all, auld Granpa had already "planted twa wives", had bought himself a new bicycle for his seventieth birthday with the proceeds of a maturing penny insurance, and had even man-aged to get himself invited along with us weans on our second stab at wartime evacuation. One way and another, not bad going for his three score years and ten and sufficient proof that he still had 'a wheen o' livin' tae dae' before getting a 'guid send-aff' to the Land o' the Leal, otherwise known as 'the ither shore.'

It must have been in the Autumn of 1940, when after our latest evacuation exile on a pig farm outside the wee toon o' Biggar, Grandpa, wee Telfie and myself were all safely gathered back into the bosom of the family, and the scene was set for Granpa to drop his own particular bombshell. There we were, a' jacose and settled that evening when just after the ritual Friday cleaning, oor wee palace was fair shining like glass. I can see it yet ... Mammy's best tea-caddy and matching brass candle-stricks had been polished up for dear life with the red velvet pad; our one and only picture, 'The Light of the World' had been flicked over with a wee bit feather duster, and the carbolic-washed Wally Dugs were sitting at a safe distance from the Westminster-chimes wedding 'knock'. We had just finished an excellent and hugely satisfying Scottish High Tea, complete with laden plates of 'pangcakes, sangwidges, sody scones' and even gargantuan slices of Mammy's famous, mouth-watering 'clootie-dumplin', and were sitting replete and in a state of stupefaction.

Yet again, as was now her wont, Mammy had reinforced her opinion and had stated for about the tenth time in as many minutes,

"Aye, Ah've said it afore and Ah'll say it again ... youse yins are a' far better aff back here in Govan wi' ma guid hamemade food in yer stomachs and facin' up tae the bombs here in Glesga, than stuck oot yonder in the wilds o' Lanarkshire, wi' no' a chip-shop in sicht. And no' tae mention yon auld skinflint o' a landlady!"

I made no reply, but with my belly fair filled tae burstin' and my jaws still going the way Ah liked them and the memory of the skimpy meals of our most recent evacuation days still fresh in my mind, I mentally agreed with Mammy. Yes, at that moment, I would not have called the King himself my cousin! And I could tell that Grandfaither too was feeling much the same, because easing his chair back from the table, he loosened his embroidered waistcoat, then slapped his ample corporation and said,

"Michty me, Janet, lass! That wis jist rerr! Mind you, Ah wonder whit ma stomach thinks o' that big tightener?"

67

There was no real answer to such a rhetorical question, but ever the right traditional, hospitable Scottish hostess, Mammy at once leapt to her feet with the words,

"It's guid tae see a man enjoyin' his grub, Grandfaither. So, ye'll manage anither wee slice o' ma clootie-dumplin', eh no, Mac?"

Quick as a flash, the auld yin was right there!

"Uch, lassie! Ye're ferr killin' me, so ye ur. But for a' that, raither than see it gae tae waste, aye! Ah'll be weel contentit for tae help ye oot."

Mind you, the fact that Daddy, sausage-curled wee bree Telfie, nor even yours truly would also have tried their best to choke down another slice or two, that idea got not a mention. Talk about the guid auld Scottish tradition of 'Family haud back!' ... 'nuff said!

Anyway, Granpa finishes his extra chunk of dumplin', then the glaikit auld stumer makes his mind-boggling announcement.

"Aye, Janet, that was lovely, hen. Therr's jist wan thing bothering me noo ... Ah'm jist hopin' that ma new wife will mak as guid a clootie-dumplin' as ma dochter-in-law!"

A stunned silence met these words, with the bold Grandfaither just sitting there, as nice as ninepence. Finally, it was left to Daddy to say,

"Your new wife, did ye say, Faither? It's the first we've heard o' ony such craitur! Who exactly micht she be, when she's at hame, like?"

Granpa cleared his thrapple and then said,

"Her name's Sarah Matilda. She's a wee widow-woman lives ower in Partick." He cleared his throat again before announcing the dénouement: "Maitter o' fact, she's a sister tae yon landlady we had in Lanarkshire."

This time Mammy was the first to recover.

"For the love o' God, Granpa! Ye're tellin' us that ye plan to wed 'Meanie Maggie's' sister! Weel, Ah jist hope for your sake, that Sarah-whitever-her-name-is, isnae an auld skinflint like yon ither miserable miser. Talk aboot making every farthing a prisoner! Hmph!"

Not the least bit 'pit-oot', Granpa just chuckled;

"Weel, a' Ah kin tell youse is that the lady's very 'weel-gaith-ered'. Her dear-departed man was a gaffer, bowler-hat and a', in John Broon's Shipyaird. She's real cosy and comfy in her ain wee room-and-kitchen, nae less, ower in Partick, in Dumbarton Road. So therr! Youse kin a' put that bit information in yer clae-pipes and smoke it! Aye, Ah'm goin' up in the world in ma auld age and don't youse forget it!"

It was Daddy's turn to laugh and look as if he'd just seen the light. He slapped his thigh in delight:

"Partick! So that's it! Ye had me fair worried there for a wheen o' months. Ye've been scuttlin' back and forth on the Govan Ferry that much, like a demented yo-yo, that Ah was beginning for tae think ye had delusions o' grandeur in your auld age! Ah thought mibbe ye seen yersell as the Captain o' the Govan Ferry! And here a' the time, ye auld devil, whit were ye daein'? Ye wis daein' a wee bit o' winchin' wi' the bride o' Pertick?"

It would have been a week or so later when Mammy invited the 'promised' couple over for a wee betrothal High Tea. If we had thought 'Meanie Maggie' was stingy, well, compared to the Bride o' Partick, our Lanarkshire landlady was your original Fairy Godmother! You'll no doubt get my meaning when I tell you that when Granpa's 'intended' sailed into our gleaming cooncil-hoose, she arrived bold as brass and empty-handed! She brought with her not so much as a crumb of a 'wee bit mindin'. Dirt-poor we McCrackens might be, but even us yins knew far better than to arrive as an invited guest at anyone's home without so much as a wee poke o' toffee-balls as yer essential 'admeet-ance-ticket.' Ah mean tae say, it's wan o' oor great auld Scottish traditions, is it no?

But even worse was to follow when we were sitting at our sump-tuous High Tea and the auld skinflint o' a bride-to-be, was getting wired intae the beanfeast, as if there was to be nae tomorrow! And between mouthfuls, she would come out, like a Greek chorus, with the oft-repeated words;

"Fair eatin' siller, this is. Fair eatin' siller!"

The thing that stuck in my craw ... it wasnae even her money she was talkin' about! I just could not get over her mean attitude, especially given that even back in our single-end days when money was even tighter, the McCracken household had always had a reputation for being 'A guid Meat-hoose.'

Love must be blind right enough, for sweet-toothed auld Granpa, ever one to enjoy his wee tit-bits and sweet-bite dainties, just could not see that if he went ahead and married his 'intended', then such culinary delights would be a thing of the past.

The sequel was that Granpa did in fact get married for the third time and Sarah Mathilda did in fact prove to be every bit as mean as the family had both feared and predicted. At one point, when they were moving to a different flat, the auld skinflint, true to her form of keeping every bawbee a prisoner, took the handles off the doors and even the very snib off the coal-bunker! Talk about a canny Scot! That auld besom gave a whole new meaning to the word 'careful!'

But the best laugh of all was at their wedding reception. Mammy and Daddy, at great personal sacrifice and expense, organised and paid the bill for a delicious High Tea at the ultra-posh Ca'doro Restaurant in Glasgow's City centre. Throughout the meal, the not-so-blushing bride kept up her usual chorus of:

"Michty me! This is ferr eatin' guid siller," at the same time 'stuffin' her turkey' as the guid old Scottish phrase so vividly expresses it.

But if we had thought the sharing of the meal to be a total embarrassment, then worse was to follow as the evening wore on. We all trooped through the city streets to Green's Playhouse Cinema, where, again at Daddy's expense, we were to round off the big day with a double-feature film show.

Seemed like a good idea at the time! The only snag was that, unbeknown to us, our new Granny had never before in her life been in a Picture Palace or Theatre of any kind and thus was unaware that the tipped-up seat should have been folded down before she sat on it! Engrossed in the film as we all were, we were in blissful ignorance of the fact that the bride, wedding-hat and all, was sitting poised on the rim of the seat and so towering above us, and more importantly, over everyone else in the hall!

Mind you, I did wonder absently why so many people were not

only muttering that well-used Glasgow 'F'-word, but were also changing their seats with amazing frequency and rapidity!

But whatever of that, it had indeed been a strange twist of Fate which had brought into our lives this 'new', if very old-fashioned Granny. Had it not been for our second attempt at evacuation, then Granpa would never have met his latest love when she chanced to spend some time down on the farm with our landlady, 'Meanie Maggie.'

Certainly an intriguing sequel to our wartime days. But as a family, we were inclined to blame it all, not on the Auld Yin himself, but rather more on Adolf Hitler!

MAMMY WAS BLACK-AFFRONTIT!

Throughout the early years of my childhood, and during all the time that we lived in the single-end, the Festival of Christmas scarcely ever got a mention. True, we were a good-living, go-to-Church-on Sundays, God-fearing family, and yet the greatest event of the Christian calendar went not only unheralded, but in fact, virtually un-noticed!

However, that was the way things were in the Scotland of the 1920's and 1930's. The great pagan festival of Hogmanay was always well and truly celebrated; the annual Glesga Fair, the somewhat Bacchanalian exodus from the City, was aye a 'rerr-terr'; yes! even Hallowe'en was an excuse for a knees-up, more commonly known in Scotland as a "wee bit o' a ceilidh".

But as for Christmas, the general attitude - at least at our social level - seemed to be that it was something to do with England and the pan-loaf speaking English ... and as such, was of no concern to true Scots! Strange logic indeed! But I can only tell it the way it was!

However, by the early 1940's that attitude was gradually changing. In the normal way, it can be difficult, if not wellnigh impossible, to pinpoint exactly when new traditions entered one's life and old habits, customs and beliefs died away.

In the case of the McCracken family and the whole new world of Christmas festivities, I know exactly the day and date! It was when a certain Polish army officer came into our lives, and exquisite manners, hair-pomade, clicking-heels and all, brought his traditions with him.

In the way of so many generous-hearted Scottish families, during wartime days, we had 'adopted' one of our noble allies. This meant that on his free days, he would come and share a traditional Scottish High Tea with us at our new coonaill-hoose.

As the month of December approached that particular year, Hela announced, in what was obviously a previously-rehearsed speech, that to repay our hospitality, at least in some measure, he would provide a small Christmas tree. Personally, we weans just couldnae see what all the fuss was aboot ... after all, Daddy already had plenty o' wee bushes - and raspberry and goosegogs ones at that - in the patch of garden which went with the territory of cooncil-hoose occupancy.

Anyway, when Hela arrived one Saturday afternoon, with the usual bowing, scraping and clicking of heels, he presented Mammy with a small pine-tree in a pot, a box of fir-cones and a packet of marzipan fruits. Leaving this little lot with us, he then decided to take a walk before tea-time.

Now, in wartime days, an entire packet of marzipan fashioned into tiny apples, oranges and bananas - anyway, who had seen a banana, fake or otherwise in years? - was something of a rarity, a real nine-days wonder!

With the wonderful inbuilt 'knowing' of children, my wee bree, Telfie, and I soon sussed out that while the fir-cones would be inedible, as to the multi-coloured 'dainties', that was an entirely different matter! And in those hard times, even Mammy herself needed no second prompting from us weans to divi-oot the spoils. In less time than it takes to tell, Telfie, Mammy and yours truly were all chomping away happily at the marzipan delights, "oor jaws goin' the wey we liked them" ... to use the guid auld Glesga expression!

The hour of reckoning came later that very same evening. No! I had not guzzled my greedy way into a bilious attack, nor had Telfie, in his usual fashion, overstuffed his mouth to the point of choking. But for all that, the disaster was there!

The moment of truth came when Hela, in his fractured and already Glesga-accented English, together with a wild display of miming, indicated that he wanted to find the previously-deposited pack of marzipan fruits.

However, by much pointing of forefingers to open gubs, followed by an exaggerated rubbing of swollen bellies, we in turn, pantomimed to indicate that not only were the delicacies finished, the delightful sweet-bites had been much enjoyed by all.

At this point, when his stunned disbelief, frustration and finally, fury, erupted into a sporadic burst of what I imagined to be Polish, I was glad not to be bilingual! Although, come to think of it, no doubt I would have learned a few words outwith the confines of any dictionary relating to the Polish language!

As you, dear readers, have already guessed ... Hela had painstakingly collected the precious, bright-coloured marzipan-fruits, and that after many months, not so that we sweet-toothed McCracken family could guzzle the lot at one sitting ... they had been intended for an entirely different purpose. Yes! That's right! His master-plan had been to decorate the Christmas tree in a very tasteful manner with the colourful, but now gone-for-ever confections!

Ah! Well! As we often say in Glesga ...

"It's nae loss whit a freen gets! And onywey, surely a thing's no' lost if ye ken where it is!"

And let's face it, we'd never before in our lives had a Christmas tree, far less even seen marzipan dainties, so how were we supposed tae ken the ins-n-oots o' the whole caboodle? Ah mean for tae say ... use yer loaf, Mac!"

TEENAGERS HADNAE BEEN INVENTED!

At the end of 1941, I attained my thirteenth year of life and became what nowadays would be termed a 'teenager.' However, in those days 'teenagers hadnae been invented', and nor had the vast range of goods, services and ideas specially geared to this particular age-group. That being the case, if I wanted to look 'grown-up' with all the sophistication of my thirteen years, there were no special clothes to aid my transformation from gawky schoolgirl to femme-fatale! I, and millions like me, had to make do with clothes designed with the older - and dare one say it - the stouter woman in mind.

Not only that, but in this no-woman's land between childhood days and adulthood, I was just as likely to go off quite happily to a Sunday-school soiree, Temperance bun-fight or even a Hallowe'en party as to a 'heavy' date to the local Flea-pit with a 'lumber.'

As for Hallowe'en parties, they really were something else! As well as 'guising' around the doors in whichever ragged outfit I had managed to codge together, I would enter into the spirit of the event by 'dookin' for apples', and then leaping up like a half-dementit gazelle for a bite at a treacle-coated scone which was swinging from a string tied to a rafter of the Church hall.

As I gradually cast off childhood matters - 'dear old Gramps' I now called the more grown-up version of 'Grandpa' - and when the latter gave the 'bethankit' before a family high tea, I would point out that it should really be called 'The Selkirk Grace' by Robert Burns:

> 'Some ha'e meat, and canna eat.
> And some wad eat that want it;
> But we ha'e meat and we can eat,
> And sae the Lord be thankit.'

Yes! I was gradually growing up and realise now that there were times when I must have been a right wee "smarty-pants" as I aired my new-found knowledge of so many topics. But precocious or not, it would still be a few years into the future before I attained the height of every young girl's ambition ... getting 'a click.' I'll never forget my first 'heavy' date when I started out on the winchin' trail.

Courtin', going-steady, otherwise known to Glaswegians as 'winchin' was done to a set pattern in those days. There would be long walks in the local Lovers' Lane - these had the added attraction of being free-; the occasional Church Soiree when tea and fern-cakes were provided cheaply together with large dollops of Readings from the Guid Book - all it cost for such gourmet evenings was a pittance hastily shoved into the Collection Plate; the gala nicht-oot at the gilded and usually packed Palais-de-Danse; or a visit to the local flea-pit for a dose of Hollywood magic, and perhaps, when funds allowed, followed by an 'intimate' supper of hot peas and vinegar at the cheapest 'Tally-wally.'

On our picture-going dates, if money was especially tight, then it would be the cheaper seats, but on high days and holidays, we would splurge out on the 'fauteuils' in the Grand Circle. But whatever price we paid, one thing remained constant, we always headed at high speed for the back row! Even at this distance in time, and the very mention of a flicks-going date, I can still blush with the memory of it, when I recall one of life's most embarrassing moments. It happened like this ...

I had met this 'older' man at a Boy Scout Party. He was all of seventeen years, while I was then sweet sixteen and never been kissed! We hit it off, or to use the Scottish word, 'clicked' from the word 'go.' Thus the scene was set for the big romance of the century!

What made this young Scottish laddie even more of a 'catch' was the fact that he was then a Merchant Navy Officer Cadet, and as such, was entitled to wear a very snazzy uniform. In fact, if the truth be told, his proud Mammy had taken him along to Paisley's Outfitting Emporium in Glasgow's Jamaica Street and there had him kitted out like an Admiral of the Fleet! The only thing missing between his splendid get-up and that of the handsome 'Chookie-Henburgh' when dressed overall, was the Ceremonial Sword! That was how he was dressed when he arrived at the pictures on that memorable evening.

With a swagger, my pseudo-Admiral deposited on the counter of the pay-desk, a carefully-hoarded white, tissue-paper fiver. The pay-clerk momentarily too stunned to speak at seeing such a fortune before her very eyes, then sighed deeply, as if she had all the cares of the world on her shoulders. Then, after another deep breath, she half-rose from her seat and addressed not only my escort but also the waiting queue with the words, "Aw, help ma Boab! Heh! Lissen, sonnie, have ye no' got nuchin' smaller than a fiver? Onywey, whit's up wi' ye? Kin ye no' read? Ur ye glaikit or sumthin? Can ye no' tak a gander at thon notice ower therr?"

Our eyes followed her pointing finger to the large sign over in the corner of the foyer. On reading the words, each written about a foot high, I blushed painfully, while my escort, in the best romantic novels' tradition, 'paled beneath his manly tan.'

But the bully of a pay-clerk, power gone to her head and with a captive audience of would-be cinema-goers already hanging on her every word, had not yet finished with us. "Aye! That's richt, Sunshine! Ye're no' needin' yer eyes tested efter all! That's exactly whit the notice says: 'Forces Personnel TUPPENCE!'

Jim started delving frantically into the depths in that all-enveloping great-coat. With the drama all but unfolded, the queue behind us was growing somewhat restive. Finally, Jim turned to me in desperation. In reply to his mute appeal, I first of all laid on the counter my ribbon-tied box of R.S. McColl's Russian Toffees. Then with my free hand, I rummaged around inside my new beaded handbag before eventually whipping out a handful of coppers. After what seemed an age of embarrassment, our tickets were punched and finally chucked, with little or no ceremony, across the counter at us.

Negotiations completed, it was only then that we were free to seek the comfort, haven and blissful anonymity of the red velvet upholstered fauteuils. But, game to the last, as we prepared to leave the foyer, we were not spared hearing one last sniesty comment from a disgruntled would-be picture-goer, right at the back of the queue:

"If that's whit's fechtin the war, God help us all. The high seas? Couldnae fecht his wey oota a paper-poke, that yin, nivver mind yer Western Approaches!"

An embarrassing experience! But at least when Ah married my brave sailor-lad years later, in 1951, Ah made sure Ah got ma money back! As for the Sea of Matrimony ... so far, it's been quite a voyage!

Finally, the reader will be aware that in telling of my 'big romance', I have skipped a few years beyond the cut-off point of 1941, the year which to me, signalled the end of childhood. However, since so many memories of my Glasgow childhood had to do with the magic of Hollywood, enjoyed in the Picture Palaces and Flea-pits of Glasgow, then I felt it only right to finish with yet one more anecdote of picture-going days.

My sincere hope is that the reader has enjoyed this "wee dauner doon memory lane" when, despite being 'deprived' of material things, we had loving parents, a secure homelife and as we Glaswegians are wont to say:

"Life was a real belter! And we nivver died a winter yet!"

SATURDAY MATINEE

When I was a child sixty years ago
Saturday afternoons were for dreaming
There in the dark of the local flea pit
with ill-shod feet propped up
on the seat in front
and a wary eye open for the usherette and her torch -
we would suck gob-stoppers, oranges, and tangerines
spit the orange-pip bullets
at the young lovers in the back row
where all too often
there was more action going on
Than up on the screen itself!
Even so, as cowboys, gangsters, maidens-forlorn
we pretended we lived
in the magic world of Hollywood
rather than in the hell-hole
that was Glasgow in the Thirties
Thus we survived the days, the months, the years
of the Depression
And with the background of loving parents
and a poor, yet cosy single-end
and in the innocence of youth
we grew to become decent citizens
unaware we were deprived
But always -
Saturday afternoons were for dreaming.

ABOUT THE AUTHOR

JENNY CHAPLIN, a freelance writer for more than forty years, lives in Rothesay. Her historical articles, features on the craft of writing and collections of poetry have been published world-wide, most recently in U.S.A., Canada and the Canary Islands. For nine years, she was the editor/proprietor/publisher of *The Writers' Rostrum*, an international literary quarterly magazine which helped many aspiring authors on the road to fame. Born in Glasgow in 1928, Jenny was brought up in the Govan district of the City, about which she has written in many of her books, most recently in *Tales of a Glasgow Childhood* (BUSINESSLIKE Publishing, 1994.)

Other books by this author include:

A Glasgow Hogmanay} (PREMIER PUBLICATIONS,
Adrift in Rothesay } Rothesay)
Alone in a Garden (KINNON ENTERPRISES, Winnipeg, Canada)
One Editor's Life (WRITERS' OWN PUBLICATIONS)
Happy Days in Rothesay (BUSINESSLIKE Publishing 1995)
From Scotland's Past (BUSINESSLIKE Publishing 1996) etc.